Roads
to
Trails

NORTHWEST
WASHINGTON

Mount Baker–Snoqualmie National Forest

Roads to Trails

NORTHWEST WASHINGTON

Mount Baker–Snoqualmie National Forest

Washington Trails Association
Coordinated by Ira Spring

THE MOUNTAINEERS BOOKS

Published by
The Mountaineers Books
1001 SW Klickitat Way, Suite 201
Seattle, WA 98134

First edition, 2002

Published simultaneously in Great Britain by Cordee, 3a DeMontfort Street, Leicester, England, LE1 7HD

Manufactured in the United States of America

Editor: Christine Clifton-Thornton
Cover Design: The Mountaineers Books
Book Design and Layout: Marge Mueller, Gray Mouse Graphics
Mapmaker: Gray Mouse Graphics
Photographer: Bob and Ira Spring, except as noted

Cover photograph: *Mount Rainier from Huckleberry Ridge, Hike 62*
Frontispiece: *Mount Garfield from the Quartz Creek road/trail, Hike 55*

A catalog record of this book is on file at the Library of Congress.

CONTENTS

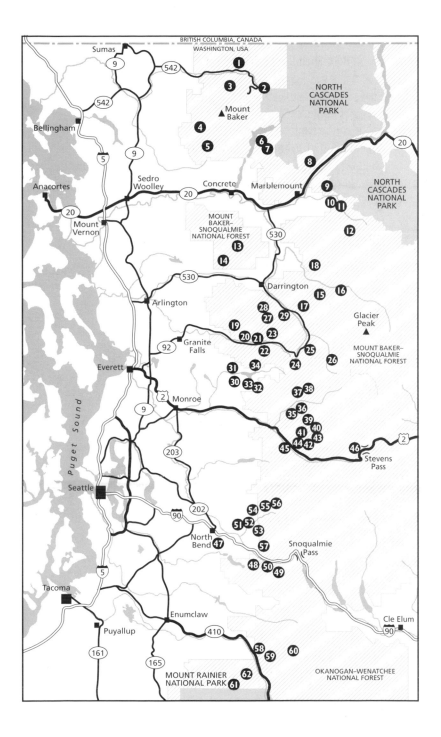

North Bend Ranger District

White River Ranger District

LEGEND			
▬▬▬	paved road, highway	90	Interstate highway
▪▪▪▪▪	improved road	2	US highway
═══	unimproved road	530	state highway
=======	primitive road	61	county road
▪▪▪▪▪▪	hiked road-trail	38	primary forest road
══╪══	gate	2040	secondary forest road
▪▪▪▪▪▪▪	hiked trail	(3800)036	forest road spur
- - - - -	other trail	697	trail number
··········	hiked route	∼∼∼	stream or river
Ⓢ	hike start point	⊣⊢⊢	waterfall
+++++	railroad	▬	lake
▲	campground	✹ ✹ ✹	marsh, swamp
◧	viewpoint	介	lookout
╥	picnic area	▲	summit
✕	mine	) (	pass

FOREWORD

RECLAIM LOGGING ROADS, INCREASE THE TRAIL SYSTEM

Once the tall trees were cut, limbed, and stacked, bulldozers ripped the ground and pushed aside stumps, dumping dirt down hillsides, burying saplings and huckleberry bushes. Tons of crushed rock formed another dusty mile of logging road, obliterating a well-loved trail. This scenario has played out time and time again in our national forests. Now is the time to reverse the damages of trail-to-road construction. We have too many roads in our national forests. We have too few trails. Let's convert some of the roads to trails.

The roads-to-trails idea was hatched by the Sierra Club during the development of the Mount Baker–Snoqualmie National Forest plan almost twenty years ago. Conservationists identified numerous logging roads that could be converted to trails, to bring the trail system back up to the mileage it had in the early 1940s. The Forest Service adopted a few of the proposals, such as at the end of the North Fork Skykomish road. Now activists are proposing road-to-trail projects in all the national forests in Washington. A small reduction in road mileage could provide a dramatic increase in trail mileage. The road system of our national forests in Washington has grown to over 20,000 miles, and the Forest Service can't afford to maintain that large a network. But trails have dwindled to about 10,000 miles, spread across seven national forests. A well-planned road system can eliminate many side roads and spurs, while fully providing for public recreation, administration, and fire management.

Converting roads to trails helps to restore watersheds and ancient forests. Roads cause erosion and impact streams and water quality. In many cases the dirt and rock excavated for the road is cast over the side, leaving another steep, erosion-prone slope below the road. This "side-cast" often gets washed downward during spring snowmelt. Roads not only destroy forests but also fragment them, substantially reducing their ecological integrity. High road densities are detrimental to wildlife. Weeds, fires, vandalism, and poaching all are more prevalent along roads. We must stop the damage and begin the restoration.

Low-elevation trails were big victims of the road construction binge in the 1950s, 1960s, and 1970s. Many hikers drive past rivers, never

Shelf Lake Falls, Hike 14

knowing the joys of the river and low-elevation forest, always going for the summit, the pass, the high lake. And with reason: Roads climbed far up the slopes, making the high country easily accessible. In addition, there is the "end of the road" syndrome—the best must be at the end of the road. Not coincidentally, much of the areas included in designated Wilderness areas in Washington State is in this higher realm, while deep forests of the lowlands have been denied this most protective of public land designations. Now we have the chance to regain trails along valley bottoms and rivers. Not only will this create more trail opportunities, but more opportunities for year-round trail use—more trails that can be used when the high country is snowed in. Low-elevation trails are often not as steep as those in the high country, and wind through forests that are more resilient than the fragile alpine vegetation. Thus, more users can enjoy them without damage.

The number of people on the trails is increasing, but the trail system is not growing. Converting roads to trails will provide many more opportunities for all types of trail users—hikers, equestrians, bicyclists, and wheelchair users. Each trail will be designed carefully for its particular attractions and users. And this important work will provide skilled jobs in rural communities. While just gating an unneeded road might suffice in some instances, we need to work to fully reclaim many roads. Pulling out old metal culverts is important, as they often get blocked and release torrents of mud during rainstorms. This returns streams to their previous channels and provides a more natural path for the trail. Pulling cast-aside material back up to the road surface leaves a more natural slope and provides soil for replanting trees and a softer trail surface. With a little extra effort, we can turn these roads into true trails.

While land managers such as the U.S. Forest Service and Washington Department of Natural Resources have pursued some projects, volunteers have been key to making this a reality. Mountains to Sound Greenway, Washington Trails Association, and Sierra Club have all helped, with volunteers planting trees and restoring creeks, planning new projects, seeking funding, and urging the agencies to do more.

Join us in that effort. Leave a legacy of more trails for the next generation.

Charlie Raines
Director, Sierra Club's Cascade Checkerboard Project

TO VOLUNTEER

Sierra Club
8511 15th Avenue Northeast, Room 201
Seattle, WA 98115
(206) 523-2147

Washington Trails Association
1305 4th Avenue, Suite 512
Seattle, WA 98101
(206) 625-1367

Washington Wilderness Coalition
4649 Sunnyside Avenue North
Seattle, WA 98103
(206) 633-1992

Mountains to Sound Greenway
1011 Western Avenue, Suite 606
Seattle, WA 98104
(206) 382-5565

PREFACE

Let's face it: Although walking an abandoned logging road has its charms, it will never be equal to hiking a wilderness trail. But when the parking lots are full at Lake 22, the Barlow Pass lot is overflowing, there are seventy cars at Granite Mountain, and over 100 at the Snow Lake trailhead, these old roads-to-trails look darn good.

This project documents the abandoned logging roads in the Mount Baker–Snoqualmie National Forest that will make good destinations for hikers and bicyclists. Each one offers something of special interest, such as a view, a virgin forest, a waterfall, or a possible campsite.

Most of these trails are not easy. In the process of abandonment, culverts beneath the road have been removed, leaving deep ditches to climb in and out. Extra ditches are sometimes added to prevent use by motorcycles and other off-road vehicles (ORVs). However, these roads/trails offer early-season walking and a degree of solitude one seldom finds on a wilderness day hike.

Poring over maps with the Forest Service road supervisor, we came up with a list of about 100 abandoned roads that were possible candidates for hiking and bicycling.

Trees grow and views can be lost in ten to twenty years after a clearcut. However, there are some locations where trees haven't done well, and views may last for another thirty years. The only way to find out was to check each one out on foot.

At eighty-three years, hiking all those abandoned roads was beyond my physical ability. A notice in *Signpost Magazine* produced fifteen enthusiastic Washington Trails Association members eager to help. While I researched the easy abandoned roads myself, the volunteers took on the harder ones. We found that sixty-two out of the 100 looked good. (About one-third of the abandoned roads that we looked at were crossed off because they were either impassable due to the dense growth of willows and alders, or because the views were cut off by the new forest.)

One of the most common comments from the volunteers was the thrill of solitude. Although there are people occasionally on these roads/trails,

Hiking the abandoned Dock Butte Road 1231, Hike 5 (photo by Louanne Choy)

Susan Crowley exploring abandoned Road 6066 on the side of Alpine Baldy.
(photo by Patrick Schneider)

if you go, it is wise to bring a companion or let people at home know where you are. In fact, at the time I gave out assignments I warned the volunteers to let families know where to look for them in case there was a problem. Unlike busy wilderness trails, it could be a year or two before someone else came along.

These sixty-two trails may be the only new trails we will get for years. Between grizzly bear habitat, environmental laws, and lack of money, converting roads to trails may be the only new hiking opportunities we will get for a long time. It is essential to document them and get the information out to the public.

These are your trails to maintain. No environmental statement was made when these logging roads were bulldozed. Now, it may sound strange, but the Forest Service cannot officially convert a logging road to a low-impact trail without going through a whole bunch of environmental loops, and trail restoration costs $10,000 a mile. For this reason, most of the trails included here are unofficial and the Forest Service cannot maintain them. It is up to the users to beat back the brush that will eventually close the trail. Each and every user must carry a clipper, or, better yet, a lopper or small hand saw and know how to use it. The Forest Service cannot give the same liability support they give to volunteers who work on recognized trail maintenance.

I hope you enjoy these trails as much as we did.

Ira Spring

INTRODUCTION

ROADS TO TRAILS: A FEW TECHNICAL POINTERS

This is not your average trail guide. Indeed, the trails and roads described herein will not provide your average trail experience. Rather, roads-to-trails are journeys of possibility. They require a simple appreciation of the outdoors in any form, as well as a little imagination to picture what they could, ideally, be.

Consider a trail: It meanders. Whether it takes you to a dramatic overlook or travels alongside a rushing stream, a good trail is more than a destination. A trail reveals the landscape as it unwinds. A well-designed trail is an experience with a logic of its own, best understood by feet (or, in some cases, by hooves or spokes).

A road is a different beast. Built for transportation, many of the roads in this book were engineered to get logging trucks from Point A to Point B. They leave a sizable mark on the landscape with little regard for the nuances of the journey. While a standard trail is 2 feet wide, a logging road measures at least 12 feet in width. Structures for water control and soil stabilization utilize large culverts, retaining walls, heavy-weight bridges, and extensive drainage ditches— much more engineering than you'll find on your average trail.

The transition from road to trail has, in some cases, been relatively smooth, such as along Elliott Creek and Taylor River: The brush and vegetation has taken over just enough to close in around a single track, and the roadbed has remained intact. Yet even in the smoothest of transitions, the presence of a wide, flat roadbed and the water that collects there is often a dead giveaway.

In other cases, the transition can be more troublesome. The "side-cast" material that was excavated to create the road in the first place can remain a liability for years to come. Older roads were sometimes built on material that contained large stumps, pieces of logs, and other organic debris. Over time this material may rot, causing the road surface to subside. In the worst case, water can build up on the inside slope of the road to the point where a portion of the road cracks and fails, falling sometimes hundreds of feet in a muddy slurry. Landslides such as these cause millions of dollars in damage to roads, trails, trees, waterways, and maybe houses below. In addition, culverts left in place may plug up and blow out, scouring salmon beds below.

The roads-to-trails described in this book lie somewhere between the two denominations of "road" and "trail." Some routes the Forest Service has officially closed and has no plans to maintain beyond basic environmental mitigation. Other routes are still active roads—although seldom driven. For the purposes of this guide, the routes have been classified into four categories: *open to vehicles, closed to vehicles, decommissioned,* and *added to the trail system.*

An *open road* is still maintained to a degree. In the best cases, road maintenance involves log and rock removal, cutting back brush, regrading as needed, and an annual checking and cleaning of culverts. However, the Forest Service does not have the budget to adequately maintain its roads, so you'll likely see some neglect while exploring these routes. In the Mount Baker–Snoqualmie National Forest, the budget for road and bridge maintenance is just over $1.2 million annually. This allows the Forest Service to complete basic maintenance on the 2400 miles of roads that lace its forests. Additional expenses, such as bridge replacement, are not included in this figure. About one quarter of the bridges in the Mount Baker–Snoqualmie will need replacing in the next few years.

A *closed road* is no longer accessible to vehicular traffic, but the Forest Service hasn't ruled out using it again at some point in the future. Accordingly, the agency preserves the original roadbed (or "prism"), but eliminates those structures, such as culverts, that require high maintenance. The agency also takes some measures, as needed, to stabilize the soil to prevent landslides or erosion. Water is a heavy and powerful medium, and in western Washington soil stabilization is a never-ending challenge. Landslides and shifting soils are common where the roadbed has saturated and crumbled—or was originally built on unstable soil.

Besides landslides and surface cracking, another clear sign of a closed road is the presence of deep trenches where the agency has removed culverts. Left unmaintained, culverts will clog, creating potential for flooding, landslides, and erosion. Removing culverts creates deep trenches across the old roadbed. These average 30 feet deep and can sometimes reach up to 100 feet deep. Even the smallest trenches can leave formidable obstacles for travelers of any sort. A couple dozen of these on a short stretch of road and a hiker might have more of a scramble that he or she originally bargained for.

Finally, *decommissioned roads* are those that have been removed from the Forest Service road system. To remove a road from official inventories, the

Monte Cristo road/trail, Hike 24

Forest Service must complete a full Access and Travel Management (ATM) plan. This study looks at the road and its impacts within the context of an entire road system and sets access, soil stabilization, and hydrological priorities within a given basin. With hydrologists, biologists, and other experts weighing in, a single study will cost from $50,000 to $100,000 and may take a couple years to complete. Four of these studies were requested for fiscal year 2002, but only one received funding. For each $100,000 spent on these studies, 240 miles of road will go unmaintained that year.

Once an analysis is complete, there still remains the actual cost of road removal. Ideally, a road is fully obliterated: The slope, drainage, and vegetation are restored to a condition that resembles the area's pre-road state. Road obliteration involves heavy equipment and special materials—and can be as complicated and as involved as road construction.

Road removal can cost anywhere from $10,000 to $60,000 per mile, depending on conditions.

It is at precisely this stage, as the landscape is being comprehensively rehabilitated, that trails would logically enter the picture as a permanent and official feature. While the Forest Service examines the long-term environmental impacts of vehicular access, it could at the same time weigh the possibility of recreational traffic. And, while the entire slope is rehabilitated, it would make sense to bring in a trail designer who could place an attractive and environmentally sensitive recreational route to follow or parallel the original road.

Low-elevation, flat roads are easiest to convert to trails and are often suitable for multi-use. There is relatively little side-cast (the fill material left over from construction) and fewer concerns of erosion. Higher elevation roads pose more concern for erosion, especially on the wet side of the Cascades.

And of course, it doesn't always make sense to replace a road with a trail. Sometimes the road went nowhere that a hiker or mountain biker would find attractive. Other times it would be easier to engineer the trail in another location, or via another route. There also may be conservation priorities that would be better served by complete environmental restoration.

After decades of construction, followed by years of under-funded maintenance budgets, the Forest Service is now actively trying to reduce its road network. Unfortunately, it takes funding and personnel to complete the environmental studies and planning needed for good road obliteration, especially if road-to-trail conversions are to be considered in the mix. Without this kind of comprehensive examination of how best to convert road closures into recreation opportunities, hikers, mountain bikers, and others have been left with a hodge-podge of roads in various states of neglect, abandonment, and obliteration.

With better funding and more support for road-to-trail conversions, agencies could do a better job of identifying priorities for new recreational routes. With official support and funding, and once compliance with environmental regulations can be ascertained, the opportunities described as trails in this guide could then be reconstructed as trails and receive maintenance. This in turn would allow these routes to handle heavier use, providing a scenic release valve for the scores of cars you'll find overflowing from many trailheads on any given summer weekend.

Elizabeth Lunney
Executive Director, Washington Trails Association

Wildlife and Human Impacts

Here in the Pacific Northwest we are blessed with an amazing number and variety of wildlands. Many of them are described in this book. We need wild places to soothe our souls and help us keep the craziness of our lives in perspective. We are also fortunate to have a tremendous diversity of wildlife, and their very presence tells us much about the health of our wildland ecosystems. As an adventurer and scientist, I have traveled around the globe to learn about wildlife in wildlands. Each time I return to my home in the Cascades I am reminded of how fortunate we are. As a scientist I have also realized the fragility of many of these ecosystems, and the plant and animal life that they support. Studies have now shown that seemingly harmless activities such as hiking can have unforeseen effects on the wildlife that rely on wildland ecosystems. However, there are many things that we can do to minimize the potential negative effects to wildlife. I offer you a few simple suggestions based on my observations:

- Keep human food out of reach of wildlife, and especially don't feed them!
- Respect wild animals' sense of space by not approaching too close and maintaining a safe distance while observing or photographing them.
- If you bring your dog on a hike, keep it on a leash and under control.
- Follow trail closures that are designed to reduce disturbance to important habitats during critical times of the year for wildlife. These usually affect small areas for short time periods, but can greatly reduce our impacts.
- Keep alert and aware of your surroundings while hiking so that you can react appropriately to a sudden encounter with wildlife.
- Finally, acknowledge the effects that hiking can have on wildlife and work with trail designers and land managers to integrate these issues early on in the design of our hiking trails. This is perhaps our most powerful tool.

We all love our wildlands and enjoy seeing the wildlife that live there. By venturing out into the remote places described in this book, we gain a better understanding and appreciation for the ecosystems necessary for the survival of many of our wildlife species. I believe it to be absolutely necessary, for us and for future generations, to have access to these wildlands. Through their enjoyment we become better citizens for our environment. By taking a little care about how we behave in our wildlands, we can pass on a legacy for our children and conserve the wildlife that we so enjoy seeing during our adventures.

Bill Gaines
U.S. Forest Service Wildlife Biologist

HEALTHY TRAILS MAKE HEALTHY PEOPLE

This book does more than describe paths to beautiful destinations in the Cascade Mountains. It also offers paths to good health.

Physical activities such as walking and hiking improve physical and mental health, reduce risk of major diseases including heart disease, high blood pressure, diabetes, obesity, and colon cancer, and increase longevity. The U.S. Surgeon General recommends people of all ages include a moderate amount of physical activity in their daily routine. On at least 5 days of the week, people should expend at least 150 to 200 additional calories daily by performing moderate-intensity activities such as walking.

But during the twentieth century, Americans became less and less physically active. Currently, 30 percent of adults are completely sedentary during

Washington Trails Association work party (photo by John Howell)

their leisure time, and another 30 percent to 40 percent are minimally active. Preventable diseases, such as obesity and diabetes, are increasing dramatically. In the last decade, there was a 61 percent increase in the percentage of Americans who are obese (12 percent to 19.8 percent), and a 49 percent increase in the percentage of Americans who have diabetes (4.9 percent to 7.3 percent). In 1999, over 13 percent of children ages 6 to 11 were overweight.

But as we encourage Americans to be more physically active, we also should provide them with ample opportunities to be active. We need communities with "physical activity friendly" environments. Part of the solution is building and maintaining the marvelous recreational trails described in this book.

I hope the hikes in this book become part of your pursuit of an active lifestyle. While most of these hikes exceed a moderate amount of activity, the good news is you gain additional health benefits through greater amounts of activity. When you aren't in the backcountry, integrate physical activity into your daily life. There are innumerable, enjoyable ways to be active, from biking to work, walking a golf course, and playing sports to gardening, kayaking, and dancing, and many, many other pleasant ways to become fit and healthy.

> David M. Buchner, MD, MPH
> Chief, Physical Activity and Health Branch
> Division of Nutrition and Physical Activity
> Centers for Disease Control and Prevention

How to Use This Book
This book describes broad, smooth, well-marked, heavily traveled, ranger-patrolled paths safe and simple for little kids and elderly folks with no mountain training or equipment, but these roads/trails and their solitude have their own brand of hazards. Treat them with the same respect you would give to a wilderness hike.

MAPS
Each hike description in this book lists the appropriate maps: Green Trails maps, the national forest recreation maps, are quite accurate, up-to-date, and inexpensive but may not show a road/trail. The best Forest Service maps are the Ranger District maps sold only at the district offices.

CLOTHING AND EQUIPMENT

Most roads/trails described in this book can be walked easily and safely, at least along the lower portions, by any person capable of getting out of a car and onto his feet, and without any special equipment whatever.

To such people we can only say, "Welcome to walking—but beware!" Northwest mountain weather, especially on the ocean side of the ranges, is notoriously undependable. Cloudless morning skies can be followed by afternoon deluges of rain or fierce squalls of snow. Even without a storm a person can get mighty chilly on high ridges when—as often happens—a cold wind blows under a bright sun and pure blue sky.

No one should set out on a Cascade trail lacking warm long pants, wool (or the equivalent) shirt or sweater, and a windproof and rain-repellent parka, coat, or poncho. (All these in the rucksack, if not on the body during the hot hours.) And on the feet—sturdy shoes or boots plus wool socks and an extra pair of socks in the rucksack.

As for that rucksack, it should also contain the Ten Essentials, found to be so by generations of members of The Mountaineers, often from sad experience:

1. Extra clothing—more than needed in good weather.
2. Extra food—enough so something is left over at the end of the trip.
3. Sunglasses—necessary for most alpine travel and indispensable on snow.
4. Knife—for first aid and emergency firebuilding (making kindling).
5. Firestarter—a candle or chemical fuel for starting a fire with wet wood.
6. First-aid kit.
7. Matches—in a waterproof container.
8. Flashlight—with extra bulb and batteries.
9. Map—be sure it's the right one for the trip.
10. Compass—be sure to know the declination, east or west.

LITTER AND GARBAGE AND SANITATION

Ours is a wasteful, throwaway civilization—and something is going to have to be done about that soon. Abandoned roads are notorious dumping grounds; fortunately, one seldom finds even a gum wrapper a hundred feet from the road-end. Meanwhile, it is bad wildland manners to leave litter for others to worry about. The rule among considerate hikers is: *If you can carry it in full, you can carry it out empty.*

Thanks to a steady improvement in manners over recent decades, and the posting of wilderness rangers who glory in the name of garbage-collectors, American trails are cleaner than they have been since Columbus landed. Every hiker should learn to be a happy collector.

On a day hike, take back to the road (and garbage can) every last orange peel and gum wrapper.

On an overnight or longer hike, burn all paper (if a fire is built) but carry back all unburnables, including cans, metal foil, plastic, glass, and papers that won't burn.

Don't bury garbage. If fresh, animals will dig it up and scatter the remnants. Burning before burying is no answer either. Tin cans take as long as forty years to disintegrate completely; aluminum and glass last for centuries. Further, digging pits to bury junk disturbs the ground cover, and iron eventually leaches from buried cans and "rusts" springs and creeks.

Don't leave food for the next travelers; they will have their own supplies and won't be tempted by "gifts" spoiled by time or chewed by animals.

Especially don't cache plastic tarps. Weathering quickly ruins the fabric, little creatures nibble, and the result is a useless, miserable mess.

Keep the water pure. Don't wash dishes in streams or lakes, loosing food particles and detergent. Haul buckets of water off to the woods or rocks, and wash and rinse there. Eliminate body wastes in places well removed from watercourses; first dig a shallow hole in the "biological disposer layer," then, if the surroundings are absolutely nonflammable, touch a match to the toilet paper (or better, use leaves), and finally cover the evidence. So managed, the wastes are consumed in a matter of days. Where privies are provided, use them.

WATER

No open water ever, nowadays, can be considered certainly safe for human consumption. Any reference in this book to "drinking water" is not a guarantee. It is entirely up to the individual to judge the situation and decide whether to take a chance.

THEFT

A quarter century ago theft from a car left at the trailhead was rare. Equipment has become so fancy and expensive, so much worth stealing, and hikers so numerous, their throngs creating large assemblages of valuables, that theft is a growing problem at busy trailheads. However, the professionals who do most of the stealing mainly concentrate on cars at popular trailheads, and, so far, cars at these seldom-used trailheads have not been targeted.

Rangers have the following recommendations.

First and foremost, don't make crime profitable for the pros. If they break into a hundred cars and get nothing but moldy boots and tattered T-shirts they'll give up. The best bet is to own a second car—a "trailhead" car: Arrive in a beat-up 1960 car with doors and windows that don't close and leave in it nothing of value. If you insist on driving a nice new car, at least don't have mag wheels, tape deck, and radio, and keep it empty of gear. Don't think locks help—pros can open your car door and trunk as fast with a picklock as you can with your key. Don't imagine you can hide anything from them; they know all the hiding spots. If the hike is part of an extended car trip, arrange to store your extra equipment at a nearby motel.

SAFETY CONSIDERATIONS

The reason the Ten Essentials are advised is that hiking in the backcountry entails unavoidable risk that every hiker assumes and must be aware of and respect. The fact that a trail is described in this book is not a representation that it will be safe for you. Trails vary greatly in difficulty and in the degree of conditioning and agility one needs to enjoy them safely. On some hikes routes may have changed or conditions may have deteriorated since the descriptions were written. Also, trail conditions can change even from day to day, owing to weather and other factors. A trail that is safe on a dry day or for a highly conditioned, agile, properly equipped hiker may be completely unsafe for someone else or unsafe under adverse weather conditions.

You can minimize your risks on the trail by being knowledgeable, prepared, and alert. There is not space in this book for a general treatise on safety in the mountains, but there are a number of good books and public courses on the subject and you should take advantage of them to increase your knowledge. Just as important, you should always be aware of your own limitations and of conditions existing when and where you are hiking. If conditions are dangerous, or if you are not prepared to deal with them safely, choose a different hike! It's better to have a wasted drive than to be the subject of a mountain rescue.

These warnings are not intended to scare you off the trails. Hundreds of thousands of people have safe and enjoyable hikes every year. However, one element of the beauty, freedom, and excitement of the wilderness is the presence of risks that do not confront us at home. When you hike you assume those risks. They can be met safely, but only if you exercise your own independent judgment and common sense.

PROTECT THIS LAND, YOUR LAND

The Cascade country is large and rugged and wild—but it is also, and particularly in the scenic climaxes favored by hikers, a fragile country. If man is to blend into the ecosystem rather than dominate and destroy, he must walk lightly, respectfully, always striving to make his passage through the wilderness invisible.

The public servants entrusted with administration of the region have a complex and difficult job and they desperately need the cooperation of every wildland traveler. Here, the authors would like to express their appreciation to these dedicated men and women for their advice on what trips to include in this book and for their detailed review of the text and maps.

On behalf of the U.S. Forest Service and The Mountaineers, we invite Americans—and all citizens of Earth—to come and see and live in some of the world's finest wildlands and to vow henceforth to share in the task of preserving the trails and ridges, lakes and rivers, forests and flower gardens for future generations, our children and grandchildren, who will need the wilderness experience at least as much as we do, and probably more.

A NOTE ABOUT SAFETY

Safety is an important concern in all outdoor activities. No guidebook can alert you to every hazard or anticipate the limitations of every reader. Therefore, the descriptions of roads, trails, routes, and natural features in this book are not representations that a particular place or excursion will be safe for your party. When you follow any of the routes described in this book, you assume responsibility for your own safety. Under normal conditions, such excursions require the usual attention to traffic, road and trail conditions, weather, terrain, the capabilities of your party, and other factors. Because many of the lands in this book are subject to development and/or change of ownership, conditions may have changed since this book was written that make your use of some of these routes unwise. Always check for current conditions, obey posted private property signs, and avoid confrontations with property owners or managers. Keeping informed on current conditions and exercising common sense are the keys to a safe, enjoyable outing.

The Mountaineers Books

1

ROADS 31, 3120, 3122, AND 3124
WEST CHURCH MOUNTAIN

Map: Green Trails: No. 13 Mt. Baker

Views, better views, and spectacular views of Mount Baker, Mount Shuksan, and everything in between. Each of the three spur roads has something different to offer: 3122 has nice trees, 3120 is almost to timberline, and 3124 offers a bird's-eye view of peaks ringing above and the valley below.

If you can't bear the steep hike up Church Mountain, drive or bike Road 31 to (somewhat) comparable views from the Church Ridge logging roads. The road ends near the Damfino Lakes trailhead.

Driving directions: Drive Highway 542 through the town of Glacier. Two miles past the Glacier Ranger Station, turn left on the paved Road 31, signed "Canyon Creek Road." At 2.8 miles, go right on FS 3120, with access

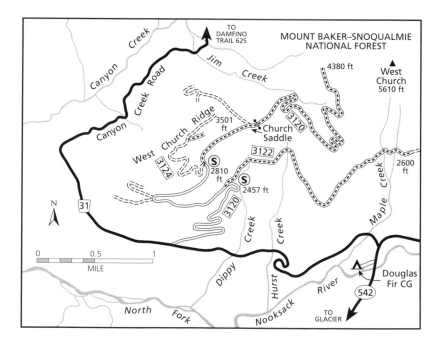

Mount Baker from West Church Ridge

to roads on Church Ridge (restricted to nonmotorized traffic from Christmas through April 15).

ROAD 3122
Road status: Closed
Round trip: 2 miles
High point: 2600 feet
Elevation gain: 150 feet

Drive FS 3120 just 1.8 miles from the paved Canyon Creek Road to FS 3122, which turns off to the right and is closed to all vehicles by a large dirt pile, elevation 2457 feet.

Alder trees provide plenty of shade. At 1 mile, the spruce trees open up to the road's best view across the valley to Mount Baker, a good turnaround point. Despite gaining several hundred feet in the first ½ mile, the level grade makes the road suitable for easy hiking along its 3-mile length. But the many blowdowns and a shallow stream crossing at about 2.5 miles make cycling difficult in parts.

ROAD 3120: CHURCH SADDLE
Road status: Under study
Round trip: 9 miles
High point: 4380 feet
Elevation gain: 1600 feet

At 3 miles from the paved Canyon Creek Road is an intersection. The most traveled road goes left and becomes 3124. FS Road 3120 continues right, elevation 2810 feet. On the way up are good views to the west, down the Nooksack Valley. At 1 mile, reach Church Saddle, elevation 3501 feet, and an open gate. A spur on the left leads to two clearcuts, the second providing the better views from the ridge south to the town of Glacier, Mount Baker, Church Mountain, and the clearcuts across the valley.

FS 3120 continues up the side of West Church Mountain to the road-end, another 3.3 miles. However, beyond the gate the road is not advised for most family cars because the Forest Service has constructed forty-two (or forty-four, I lost count) deep drainage ditches and most cars won't have the required clearance. Fireweed, pearly everlasting, and more views of Mount Baker reward those who hike or bike to the road-end at a scraped-out clearing, 4380 feet. Mountain bikers have plenty of chances to catch air on the way down, hopping the ditches.

ROAD 3124: WEST CHURCH RIDGE
Road status: Under study
Round trip: ¼ mile
High point: 3500 feet
Elevation gain: None

For great views, follow Road 3124 to its end at West Church Ridge. At its end the view is limited by trees, but drive back a short 0.2 mile and walk the first abandoned spur to a spectacular viewpoint, from Mount Baker to Mount Shuksan.

(For other enjoyable views and an easier drive, bypass 3120 and stay on Canyon Creek Road until it ends, 15.2 miles from Highway 542. The road is well maintained and well graded, and follows Canyon Creek past several campsites and then around behind Church and Bear Paw Mountains. Near the road-end is a short (0.7 mile) trail to Damfino Lakes, a lonely, shady spot with cool camps and more short hikes to views that go all the way to Canada!)

By Steve Bernheim

2 ROAD 5080
WHITE SALMON GLACIER VIEW

Road status: Gated
Round trip: 2½ miles
High point: 3800 feet
Elevation gain: 400 feet

Map: Green Trails: No. 14 Mt. Shuksan

What a view! So close to the west side of Mount Shuksan you can almost reach out and touch its hanging glaciers. As an extra benefit, you'll miss the crowds at Artist Point and maybe even have a solitude experience on this easy walk.

Driving directions: Drive the Mount Baker Highway toward Heather Meadows. Just beyond milepost 52, the highway makes a sharp turn to the right; go left and park at a gate, elevation 3574 feet.

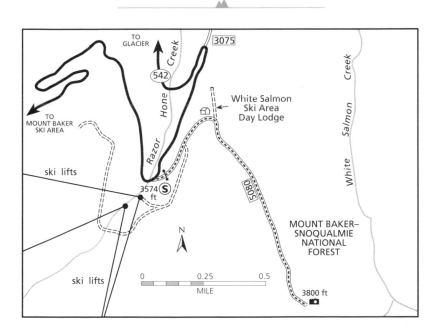

Mount Shuksan and White Salmon Glacier from end of hike

Walk past the gate into a huge parking area. In ⅓ mile, reach the White Salmon Ski Area Day Lodge. Between the day lodge and ski patrol building, find a forest road maintained for workers to access the ski area in the summertime.

The way is now in a cool forest, with tantalizing glimpses of glaciers through the trees. In 1 mile a groomed ski trail enters from the right; stay straight ahead into a clearcut at the end of the road. Find a log to sit on and dig out a map.

A thousand feet below is White Salmon Creek. At eye level is the lower White Salmon Glacier. To the right are the small glacier on Shuksan Arm, the upper White Salmon Glacier, the ice cliffs of the Hanging Glacier, and the Summit Pyramid of 9131-foot Mount Shuksan.

By Ira Spring

3 ROAD 37
THOMPSON CREEK

Road status: Closed
Round trip: 3 miles
High point: 4300 feet, at trailhead
Elevation loss: 200 feet

Map: Green Trails: No. 13 Mt. Baker

After driving 13 miles on a dirt road, why would anyone choose Thompson Creek over the spectacular views and flower-covered meadows of the nearby Skyline Divide trail?

If the Thompson Creek road/trail and its family camping opportunities were anywhere else it would get rave reviews, but it is hard to justify hiking this abandoned road while comparing it to Skyline Divide. However, when the Skyline Divide parking lot is overflowing with thirty or more cars, Thompson Creek is a good alternative.

Driving directions: Drive Highway 542 to 1 mile beyond the town of

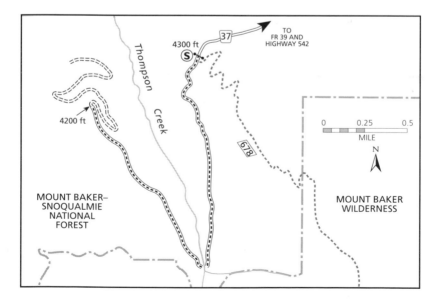

Confluence of Boundary Creek and Thompson Creek

Glacier. Turn right on Glacier Road 39, and in 100 feet go left on Road 37 for 13 miles to where the road is blocked at the Skyline Divide trailhead, elevation 4300 feet.

The moment of decision has arrived! Skyline Divide or the Thompson Creek abandoned road? This story is about hiking abandoned roads. So ignore the Skyline trail, cross the road-end barrier, and follow the old tread of the abandoned road round the first bend, out of sight and temptation, and forget all those other hikers headed for the high country.

In a few feet the way enters the Thompson Creek valley, with a view of an unnamed 6500-foot peak dead ahead and a long sweep out to the Puget Sound Country. If it were not for all those water ditches, the route would be easy, and it's so little used that some parts are covered with moss. In season, flowers line the route—paintbrush, fireweed, penstemon, and an occasional tiger lily. One side stream is covered with a mimulus and with little yellow flowers I am not familiar with.

In 1½ miles, reach the site of the former Thompson Creek bridge, replaced by a cold, 3-foot-deep ford. On the other side of the creek the road goes on another 2 miles, but this is far enough. Look around; just above the bridge site is a delightful pool and the cascading Boundary Creek pouring into Thompson Creek.

A campsite at Thompson Creek is a bit tipped, but there are nicer ones along the way at a number of streams with nearby wide spots for a tent.

By Ira Spring

4 ROAD 38
MIDDLE FORK NOOKSACK

Road status: To be open to Elbow Lake trailhead

IF ROAD IS OPEN TO TRAILHEAD
Round trip: 8 miles
High point: 3700 feet
Elevation gain: 1100 feet

IF ROAD IS CLOSED AT WALLACE CREEK
Round trip: 12 miles
High point: 3700 feet
Elevation gain: 1500 feet

Map: Green Trails: No. 45 Hamilton

As fall approaches in the Pacific Northwest, clear days for hikes with views become less and less frequent. On a mid-September Saturday, the weather forecast called for a sunny afternoon, so I left Seattle under overcast skies, hoping for the best. As I drove the 2½ hours north to the closed bridge on Forest Road 38, the skies did in fact begin to clear. Good sign, I thought.

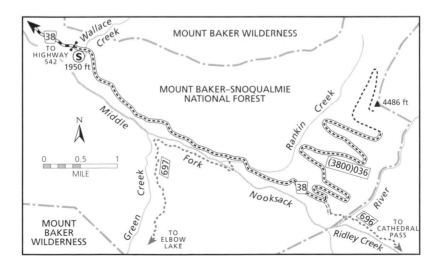

I was looking forward to the promised views of the Twin Sisters Mountain, described in geology books as a piece of rock unique on the entire continent. Dunite is normally extremely rare, and the Twin Sisters are a solid block of the stuff, giving the mountain an orange color different from other local ranges and drawing the attention of geologists from all over. It is not a form that has high commercial value, which explains why it remains remote and intact.

The great thing about this particular closed road is that it will ensure a little more solitude to those heading for the two trailheads, and for that alone it benefits the outdoor community. And the views at the top may be much better than I suspect.

Driving directions: Drive Highway 542 toward Mount Baker. Just short of milepost 17 and the hamlet of Welcome, turn right and go 5 miles on the Mosquito Lake road. At Porter Creek, go left on Road 38 for another 4.9 miles, then go left again, still on Road 38. At 9.9 miles reach Wallace Creek, where the road may be closed. If open, drive on to wherever it ends.

------------------------------------ ▲▲ ------------------------------------

Forest Road 38 winds through second-growth foothills in the vicinity of Mount Baker. It passes private forestlands still being actively logged, with recent clearcuts and warnings about truck traffic. Several houses I passed just before the beginning of the road had signs reading "This family supported by logging" displayed proudly in their driveways.

The Forest Service has clearly posted details of their road closure at mile 9.9. Cars with trailers are advised to turn back early. Other vehicles make their potholed way up to the barrier at road's end, just shy of a colorfully deteriorated wooden bridge over Wallace Creek. There were several cars parked here the day I visited, their occupants likely headed for one of the two popular trailheads up the way. The Forest Service has determined that the bridge is unsafe for vehicle traffic, and I wasn't going to argue with their verdict, given the look of the bridge. Since it is a relatively short distance beyond the bridge to the former end of the road, and given the current climate regarding road closures, I would be surprised if the road is ever reopened past this point. Elevation 1950 feet.

The view down to the rushing creek below the bridge turned out to be one of the day's highlights (unfortunately). I mounted my bike and proceeded up the road. The road is in mint condition, its wide gravel surface built to the highest Forest Service standards. The grade is gradual, passing through pleasant second-growth forest within the sound but not sight of the rushing Middle Fork Nooksack River. The sides of the road were colorful with asters and fireweed. There were no views.

Just shy of 1½ miles past the beginning of the road/trail, there is a large former parking area on the left-hand side of the road just across from the beginning of the Elbow Lake trail. I followed the trail (unmarked by any sign) a short distance down to the Nooksack River, where I stood upon the wooden bridge and marveled at the brimming muddy water, looking for all the world like a spring flood in September. Nothing like the high country to turn seasons topsy-turvy.

The road/trail continues another mile and a half. The way continues to be gradual and uneventful, with no views or special features. At road-end there is another trailhead, to Cathedral Pass. Just before this point, spur Road

Wallace Creek bridge, where four wheels are exchanged for two (photo by Gary Faigin)

36 branches off to the left. I left my bike at the beginning of the spur and headed up.

The spur road follows a switchback route over a logged-over ridge, gaining 1200 feet in elevation over 2 fairly tedious miles. I watched the overcast sky expectantly for signs of clearing. Though "sucker patches" of blue appeared now and again, the trend did not seem to be in my favor; the day grew darker. As I trudged closer to the top of the ridge, views of a sort opened up back across the valley of the Nooksack. For a moment I could see the peaks of the Sisters, then the sky closed in again.

The topographic map shows a trail continuing past the end of the spur road, and indeed I found a faint trail (probably a much clearer route before the logging) continuing up and over the embankment that marked the road-end. The trail makes its way through messy logging debris and brush, following the base of the cliffs that lead up to the ridge top. In

Alder catkins along Middle Fork road

good weather the views to the southwest of the Twin Sisters would be good; I'm not sure about views of Mount Baker to the northeast. Today there was nothing to be seen.

I continued following the trail to where the map showed a dogleg to the right. At this point the route follows the cliff base to the back of the ridge top, then makes its way up to the very crest. However, I was not able to find out what this portion of the route was like, because now the cloud layer lowered and visibility deteriorated to practically zero. It began to drizzle lightly. I retreated.

All the long way down the spur switchbacks the fog continued. Maddeningly, I could see clear sky to the west, in the lowlands, but the local storm stubbornly continued, like my own personal cloud.

I retrieved my bike and started down. Here the fun began. The wide, intact road surface, with only gentle curves, became my raceway for one of the fastest downhill rides I've had. There was no one on the road, no obstacles, and few potholes. The world whizzed by. I was back to the closed bridge in a scant fifteen minutes.

By Gary Faigin

5 ROAD 1231
DOCK BUTTE ROAD

Road status: Closed
Round trip: Estimated 4 miles (including extra mileage on approach road)
High point: 3740 feet
Elevation gain: 600 feet

Map: Green Trails: No. 45 Hamilton

This moderately graded hike offers an excellent close-up look at Loomis Mountain, as well as more distant views of Dock Butte and faraway Baker Lake. It also offers consistently deep trenches to run down, then up the other side, which was a bit punishing to the knees. Trekking poles would definitely help. We had to bushwhack through some thick stands of young deciduous trees, which were so closely knit that you had to step on some of the branches to get through. I felt bad, even knowing that I was supposed to be staking a trail.

Driving directions: Drive Highway 20 east from Sedro Woolley and between mileposts 82 and 83 go left on the Baker Lake–Grandy Lake Road 12.5 miles to the National Forest boundary. Continue another 0.2 mile and go left on FS Road 12. At 7 miles, go left again on Road 1230 for about 1 mile to Road 1231. The "maintained" road doesn't officially end until about a mile later, but after scraping bottom once in my Corolla, we parked. Only vehicles with more than a foot of clearance would be recommended to continue on to that point due to severe dips and bumps in the road.

▲▲

Between our parking place and the road's official end, it's a nice walk, well-treed with lush undergrowth, lots of animal scat in the road, and more songbirds than I've noticed in quite a while. There are several flat places to set up a car camp just off the road, some with established fire rings and thick mossy beds for tent sites.

As you approach the end of the maintained road, you get a first glimpse of Loomis Mountain, with its reefed top and bright green avalanche valleys. It was tempting to continue on straight up the meadows and blaze our way to the top, but looks can be deceiving, and the 5587-foot top wasn't nearly as close as it appeared. The road passes over Loomis Creek, which was invisible in all the thick underbrush, probably due to the fact that all but a tiny snowpatch had melted by our early September visit, but its quiet trickle was a constant presence. I would guess that in the rush of the spring snowmelt, it's a much bigger force to contend with, but for our hike, it passed under the road completely out of sight.

As the road turns to the right, it's easy to see where any semblance of maintenance ends. The trail heads eastward, gradually climbing the ridge as it tapers down and away from Loomis Mountain. As the road climbs, the valley drops away beneath to

Look for these mushrooms among the old growth trees along the abandoned road

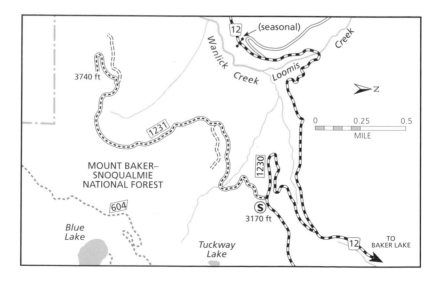

Loomis Mountain from abandoned Road 1231 (photo by Louanne Choy)

the east, creating a feeling of increased elevation gain.

There are several deep water trenches, a few landslides that look from the plant growth to be fairly old, and uneven tread almost every step of the way. At about 1½ miles in, you'll reach the largest washout, which will be obvious. Stay to the inside of the slope, near a downed tree, for stable ground and some trees and rocks to hang on to while you traverse the steep gully. At about 2 miles you'll reach the end of the road, a large flat area that looks to have been a truck turnaround—it's that big. If you can haul up enough water, it would be an excellent, but exposed, group campsite. There are unobstructed views back to Loomis, over to Dock Butte and the surrounding ridges, and back east up the valley all the way to Baker Lake and the peaks beyond.

By Kim Sharpe

6 ROAD 1107-012
SONG BIRD HAVEN

Road status: Open to ORVs
Round trip: 4 miles
High point: 3750 feet
Elevation loss: 200 feet

Map: Green Trails: No. 46 Lake Shannon

Mount Baker dominates this area but is in stiff competition with a stunning view of Mount Shuksun, a panorama of the mountains northeast of Baker, and a straight shot up the Baker River Valley. This is a good place for birdwatching. The clearing just before the end of the road is the best place to observe and enjoy our fine-feathered friends.

Driving directions: Drive the North Cascades Highway 20 east of Sedro Woolley and between mileposts 82 and 83 go left on the Baker Lake–Grandy Lake Road. Enter the Mount Baker–Snoqualmie National Forest at 12.5 miles and continue approximately 2 miles more, then turn right on the Baker Dam–Baker Campground road. In 1 mile drive over the Baker Lake Dam, and in 2 miles go left on gravel Road 1107. Follow

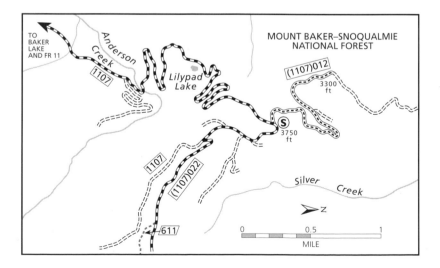

Looking up the Baker River Valley toward Whatcom Peak (photo by Tom Karchesy)

this scenic road about 8 miles to a switchback, then go left on Road (1107) 012. Park here, elevation 3750 feet.

You can drive farther, depending on how much you want to beat up your vehicle. Don't be surprised to see four-wheelers or ORVs on the road. Bear hunters favor this area during their season. Wear bright colors during that time of year. The area was clear-cut some years ago, but it is still a pleasant hike. This is an excellent road for a bike ride. The road is downhill all the way out, but not bad coming back. It is pretty much bug free, which could be because of the lack of water in the area.

Mount Baker dominates this area, but there is a stunning view of Mount Shuksan. There are a lot of good views of the mountains northeast of Baker and you have a straight shot up the Baker River Valley.

Toward the end of the trail I found a noisy community of birds. On my first visit I was standing there, marveling at the sight of Mount Shuksan, when I was startled by a *bizzz-pst* behind me. I turned to see a humming bird hovering, and then off it went with its companion. She came back to show off; went straight up and dove down, did a loop-to-loop, and off it went frolicking with its mate. Then the finches came by, likewise playing around. I couldn't help but sit there and watch these rascals in their merry-making. Then I was treated to a chorus of I-don't-know-how-many different birds.

This is a good place for birdwatchers. The clearing just before the end of the road is the best place to observe our fine-feathered friends.

By Tom Karchesy

7 ROAD 1107
FACE THE MOUNTAIN

Road status: To be closed
Round trip: 2½ miles
High point: 4300 feet
Elevation gain: 300 feet

Map: Green Trails: No. 46 Lake Shannon

The end of this road is the perfect spot to stand and face the mountain. The main road leads to the popular Watson Lake Trail, but this sideroad is a well-ignored jewel. In addition to The Mountain, you have a birds-eye view of the lower valley. This definitely has one of the best views in the area.

Driving directions: Drive the North Cascades Highway 20 east of Sedro Woolley and between mileposts 82 and 83 go left on the Baker Lake–Grandy Lake Road. Enter the Mount Baker–Snoqualmie National Forest at 12.5 miles and continue approximately 2 miles more, then turn right on the Baker Dam–Baker Campground road. In 1 mile drive over

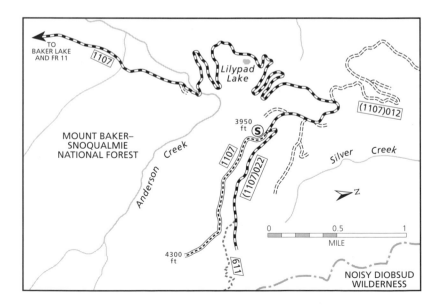

Mount Baker from abandoned Road 1107 (photo by Tom Karchesy)

the Baker Lake Dam, and in 2 miles go left on gravel Road 1107. Follow this scenic road about 9-plus miles to a junction. Go straight ahead on the abandoned road a few feet and park, elevation 3950 feet. If you are thinking of driving farther, the road is awful, with deep fissures that are starting to slide. The road is easy to walk or bike.

At the beginning of the trek are some nice views down to Shannon Lake and the Baker Lake Dam. The road has a gradual incline through a young evergreen forest. A mile down the road, you'll pass four turnouts with fire rings. In another ½ mile is a clearing on the crest of the ridge. On one side you can peer down a steep valley and wonder how they logged it without falling off. Continuing down the road for another ¼ mile brings you to a precipice with a majestic view of The Mountain. When you get here you are staring Baker in the face.

It is really nice. The best time to come here is early in the morning. It's secluded, and there is a good chance you'll see some wildlife. Just the solitude is fantastic. Relax, watch for wildlife, and at the same time observe how, as the day progresses, the shadows change the mountain. If you come later in the day, the mountain may be washed out in the bright afternoon sun. Plus, with little shade and no water supply, it can get dry and dusty on a hot day.

Looking below, you have a birds-eye view of the valley. You can't miss anything moving down there. Spring is the best time to view the wildlife, but any time is good enough to watch the mountain.

By Tom Karchesy

8 ROAD 1062 BACON CREEK

Road status: Closed

FIRST VIEW
Round trip: 9 miles
High point: 2800 feet
Elevation gain: 2000 feet

HIGH VIEW
Round trip: 13 miles
High point: 3800 feet
Elevation gain: 3000 feet

Map: Green Trails: No. 47 Marblemount

A report by Deborah Cooke, another volunteer, claimed that this is an undiscovered gem of an area, despite extensive logging. Because it's on the edge of wilderness, and much of it is overgrown and inaccessible, it has become de facto wilderness. There are lots of bears—the first evening

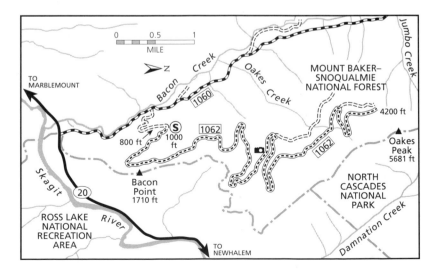

we walked a short distance up Road 1062, we saw one bear and heard two others. On our second trip up 1062, we saw lots of recent bear signs. It might be nice just to leave the area inaccessible to hunters.

Driving directions: Drive the North Cascades Highway 20 from Sedro Woolley to Marblemount, then another 4.8 miles to Bacon Creek. A few feet after crossing the creek go left on Bacon Creek Road 1060. Drive 1.4 miles and go right on Road 1062. Elevation 1000 feet.

I would repeat this trip again to give you an up-to-date report on the battle of the brush, but this isn't a trip one should do alone. I have a reputation for pushing through brush. The friend who accompanied me the first time didn't exactly jump at the chance to go again and another friend who owes me a bushwhacking trip is suddenly busy with "adult responsibilities."

On my first trip I was able to drive the first 0.5 to 0.8 mile of Road 1062 to a pullout just below where the road became impassable to vehicles due to slumping. So my description starts here. For the first mile or so the road/trail was clear and in good shape, but then we ran into the first of several thickets. A couple of these were so bad that we needed to help each other when we became pinned by the trees. So I understand why Deborah Cooke reported it impenetrable. The good news is that the overgrowth was intermittent and the road surface was in excellent shape the entire way, with little water damage.

The lower elevations of Road 1062 are completely forested—no views, but pleasant. We thought perhaps Bacon Point would afford a view if we scrambled up to it, but we couldn't even see it through the trees so we figured a bushwhack to it wouldn't be worthwhile.

The first spot with a view is at 2800 feet, about 4½ miles from where we started hiking. There are great views of the valley, and of Diobsub Buttes. Can't remember how many peaks we could see to the northwest from here. Unfortunately, the view area is maybe only 1/16 mile long and the trail is soon back in the trees. We camped at the view spot in the middle of the road. There was easily accessible water just up the road from our campsite.

The next day, the weather closed in and we had swirling clouds, rain, and lightning. We continued on up the road to the logged-off area and the final fork, and it looked like both forks would contour around the slope enough to get great views to the north and northwest. Unfortunately, it

A surprise visitor

was so overcast that we only got a couple of one-second views as the mists swirled, and we're not sure what we saw. (I think we may have even caught a glimpse of a peak to the south.) I'm pretty sure the ridge had been logged to just below the rocky part of Oaks Peak. Also, there is a saddle just to the south of Oaks Peak that would probably afford some views. It will be quite some time until the views are obscured by trees, but because the road is not on the edge of a steep slope, eventually trees will interfere.

By Anita Sterling

9 ROAD 1520 MARBLE CREEK

Road status: Closed

TO GRANITE SLAB CREEK
Round trip: 2 miles
High point: 1600 feet
Elevation gain: 400 feet

TO ROAD-END
Round trip: 5 miles
High point: 1850 feet
Elevation gain: 650 feet

Maps: Green Trails: Nos. 47 Marblemount, 48 Diablo Dam (road is not shown)

In 1966, the Marble Creek road ended in a very impressive view looking straight up into the cirque of Marble Creek and the small glaciers between 8386-foot Tepeh Towers and 8868-foot Eldorado Peak. While taking a picture I contemplated how great it would be to climb that ridge

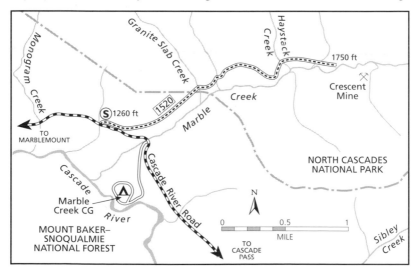

Twinflower

line. A few years later, my wife Pat and I did walk the thin, scary ridge leading to Eldorado Peak. On one side was a drop of 300 feet to a steep ice slope and the crevasse-covered Inspiration Glacier. On the other side we looked down 6000 feet into the deep hole of Marble Creek.

About 1970, the road was abandoned and dropped from the USGS and Forest Service maps. I have always thought it would be great to turn the road into a trail. This roads-to-trails project was my first opportunity.

There is no evidence of where the old road starts. I knew the road was there, but Pat and I made two futile attempts thrashing around in brush near the Marble Creek bridge without finding it. In my basement I found an old 1950s forest map and realized we'd been looking in the wrong place.

Driving directions: From Marblemount, drive the Cascade River Road some 8 miles to the Marble Creek Campground. Turn around and drive back 0.4 mile to a small parking area near a rockslide. On the north side of the road, well hidden, is the long-abandoned road, elevation 1260 feet.

▲▲

Someone is keeping the road/trail open. Except for rotting poles and sticks and an occasional tree to step over or under, the roadbed is easy to walk. In a short 1 mile, Granite Slab Creek (has no name on the USGS map) has gouged a deep hole in the road, and the road disappears in a tangle of brush and boulders. Across the creek we beat our way through heavy brush and regained the old roadbed. A path of sorts marks the way and shows some use, but there is little of the tender loving care the first mile had. Tantalizing glimpses of glaciers through the treetops kept us going. At 1½ miles, Haystack Creek has gone wild. The old roadbed is criss-crossed with big logs and gushing torrents.

Marble Creek and Eldorado Peak, from the Road 1520 road-end

While this crossing would have been a breeze for us ten or fifteen years ago, in our eighties we have slowed down and decided against undertaking the stream crossing. We went back to the granite slabs for lunch and a bit of sunbathing beside a small waterfall, so I cannot confirm whether the wonderful view I photographed at the road-end is still there.

By Ira Spring

10 ROAD 1551
IRENE RIDGE

Road status: Under study
Round trip: 2½ miles
High point: 3700 feet
Elevation gain: 450 feet

Maps: Green Trails: Nos. 47 Marblemount, 48 Diablo Dam

It would be hard to beat the views of the glaciers on Eldorado seen from the access road as it climbs 2200 feet from the Cascade River to the end of the drivable road at 3200 feet. However, walking the gated road opens up terrific views of 7435-foot Snowking Mountain.

Driving directions: From Marblemount, drive the Cascade River Road 10.1 miles. Just past the community of Sibley, go right on Road 1550 (unsigned). The road crosses the Cascade River at 0.8 mile, then in four long switchbacks and many stops for pictures, it reaches the end of the

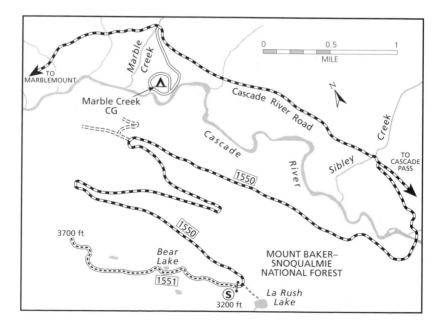

Eldorado Peak from Irene Ridge

drivable road at a gate and a parking area 7 miles from the Cascade River Road, elevation 3200 feet.

From the parking area, an obscure trail descends to La Rush Lake and climbs to Bear Lake at an elevation of 3695 feet. Both lakes are surrounded by forest.

For views, and that is what this trip is all about, walk past the gate on Road 1551. In ¼ mile is a rock quarry. Find an old bulldozer route circling around the bald knob for views north and south and into the Cascade Pass area. This would be an ideal place to spread out a map while eating lunch. But don't stop here too long, for the farther one goes, the better the views get of Snowking. The way alternates between cool forest and clearcuts, with great views above Irene Creek. The way ends in 1¼ miles, elevation 3700 feet. The end is an anticlimax, with a limited view looking down at the Cascade River and across to Lookout Mountain.

By Ira Spring

11 ROAD 1570-130
SONNY BOY CREEK

Road status: Road closed and bridge gone

TO SONNY BOY CREEK
Round trip: 1½ miles
High point: 1400 feet
Elevation gain: 200 feet

TO KINDY CREEK VALLEY
Round trip: 3 miles
High point: 1600 feet
Elevation gain: 400 feet

Map: Green Trails: No. 80 Cascade Pass

Once upon a time, not so very many years ago, this was a wonderful valley walk. There were big trees, make that huge trees, two roaring torrents, a narrow canyon, and an easy backpack hike.

Over time, the truck bridge over Kindy Creek became unsafe and the road became a great footpath. However, rotten planking gave the Forest

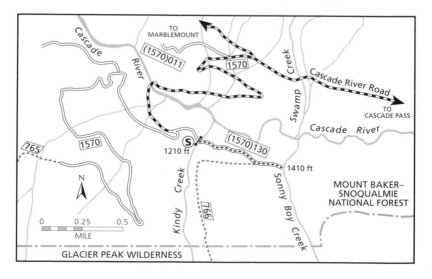

Kindy Creek

Service, who is susceptible to lawsuits, a reason to remove the bridge, leaving just one of the stringers in place. A steady person could walk the remaining stringer, but a fall to rocks or into the raging water would be serious. With the equipment the Forest Service used to remove the bridge, a hiker/bicycle bridge could have been put in place.

Driving directions: Drive Highway 20 to Marblemount, cross the Skagit River, and continue east 14.5 miles on the Cascade River Road. Turn right on Kindy Creek Road 1570, cross the Cascade River, and in 1.6 miles, keep left at a junction to Road 1570-130 and go another 0.3 mile to its end at the site of the old Kindy Creek bridge, elevation 1210 feet.

If the bridge is repaired, walk across Kindy Creek as it roars out of a narrow canyon. The road is being covered by alders, but otherwise the tread is good all the way to Sonny Boy Creek. For the Kindy Creek trail, walk some 300 to 400 feet from the site of the old bridge and take the first path to the right beyond the sandy bank. With a bit of searching, find the still-intact tread of the Kindy Creek trail and enter a grove of magnificent trees. A few are 8 feet in diameter. The way climbs steadily within sound of Kindy Creek, which is hidden in a chasm. In a long mile the trail ends in a massive flood area, which took out the tread that used to go for miles up the valley.

By Ira Spring

12 ROAD 16
JORDAN RIDGE

Road status: To be closed at Slide Lake trailhead
Round trip: 9½ miles
High point: 4440 feet
Elevation gain: 1680 feet

Map: Green Trails: No. 79 Snowking Mtn.

Great views of distant mountains and nearby peaks, access to a fishermen's path to remote lakes, and the chance to hike in an area with a dearth of established trails all contribute to making this road a worthwhile jaunt. In some places stands of large old-growth trees make the foreground a pleasant experience as well. Take note that the road extends about twice as far as shown on the 1982 USGS map; the Green Trails and Ranger District maps both show the new road length.

Driving directions: From SR 530, just north of milepost 65 and about

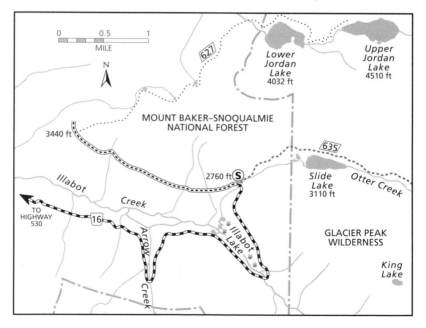

A big tree on a hillside along Road 16 (photo by Eric Cook)

2 miles south of Highway 20, turn east onto the well-maintained gravel road signed "Illabot Creek Road (FS Road 16)." Drive 21 miles to the Slide Lake trailhead, where a sign warns that the road beyond will soon be closed. Park here, elevation 2760 feet.

The first 2 miles are a long, steady climb west, up the side of the valley. New and old clearcuts to the left, though not themselves very visible, leave plenty of viewing opportunities for many decades to come. The rock and ice summit of Mount Chaval appears to the southeast early in the hike. The Illabot Peaks, not much to look at on the map, provide a constantly improving sight of waterfalls, rocks, and meadows off to the left. Just before the 2-mile point the road passes through a wide swath of logging and through an interesting stand of burnt and silvery snags.

The road then turns to the north and makes a large, steep switchback. When the views disappear, the patches of old growth appear. Large, straight trees decorated with strands of bright-green moss crowd in on the road, providing a nice relief to the constant tree-harvested foreground. It's about 3 miles from the parking lot that a sidetrail can be found. Those with a hankering for boot-beaten, fairy-tale faint fishermen's paths can find the start to the right of a gatepost (the road was not gated here on our survey), just before the road dips to cross a sizable stream at 4080 feet. This way trail through beautiful woods eventually reaches the pretty Jordan Lakes, but is not maintained and is difficult to follow in many places.

Ever upwards the road continues for another 1¾ miles, with mixed views of faraway mountains. After a major washout at 4400 feet, the road levels off significantly, continuing west and north to the roads' end just past a giant pile of old logs. Here are obscured views north to Mount Baker and the Picket Range. To the west is a clear view of the Skagit Valley.

This is a hike where the views are great throughout, even if you don't go all the way to the end of the road. And while the sidetrail to Jordan Lakes might not be within every person's abilities, everyone should peer into the ancient forest and back a few thousand years.

By Eric Cook

13 ROAD 1735
FINNEY PEAK

Road status: Road closed by slide
Round trip: 6 miles
High point: 5083 feet
Elevation gain: 1600 feet

Maps: Darrington Ranger District and Green Trails: Nos. 77 Oso, 78 Darrington

An imposing lookout site on top of a rocky point. When built in 1933, the lookout was reached by a 15-mile trail. In 1968, when it first appeared in our *100 Hikes in Western Washington* book, the trail had been shortened to 8 miles. Logging roads chewed up the trail until, in 1970, when the first edition of *101 Hikes in the North Cascades* was published, only 2½ miles were left. However, by the second edition, in 1979, the trail was lost in a tangle of logs, stumps, and waist-high brush. I poked around and, by hiking a half mile of an abandoned spur road with a short climb through a stand of trees, I discovered the last half mile of trail was still useable. Since then I have been given a copy of the Forest Service's

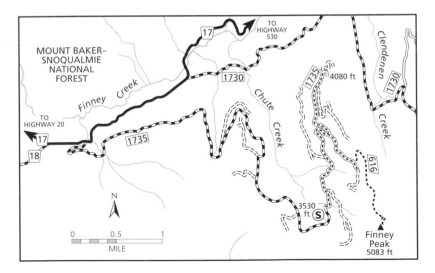

directive, which states that the loggers were to restore the trail when the cutting was finished. But the left hand doesn't always listen to the right hand, and nothing has been done. The views are still there and are no longer blocked by all those old, dying, mature trees.

Driving directions: There are two ways to reach Finney Peak. From I-5, drive State Highway 530 toward Darrington. Near milepost 44, go left on Swede Heaven Road about 1.5 miles, and then go right on FS Road 18. Climb over the pass and down the Finney Creek Valley to Road 1735. Go left another 5.7 miles to the road end.

Whitehorse Mountain from Finney Peak

The preferred way is mostly paved. On Highway 20, drive to the west side of the town of Concrete and turn right on the Skagit–Sauk River–Concrete County Road. Cross the Skagit River, turn left, and drive about 9 miles. Turn right on FS Road 17. At 13 miles from the Skagit–Sauk River–Concrete County Road, go left on Road 1735 for another 5.7 miles, to where a small unnamed creek has left a gaping hole in the road, elevation 3530 feet.

A footpath has been cut around the gap made by the creek, and in a short half mile an unstable mudslide must be crossed. Except for these two problems, the road, carpeted with clover, is easy to walk.

In 1 mile, reach a Y and go left along an abandoned spur to its end. Climb up some 250 feet in a patch of virgin timber and near the ridge top find what remains of the original trail to the peak. The last few feet are blasted to the 5083-foot site of the Finney Peak Lookout.

In addition to clearcuts, there are views north to Mount Baker, the Pickets, White Horse Mountain, and a page full of other peaks up and down the Cascades.

By Ira Spring

14 ROAD 1840
SHELF LAKE FALLS AND HAWKINS LAKE

Road status: Closed
Round trip: 3½ miles
High point: 3650 feet
Elevation gain: 450 feet in, 125 feet out

Maps: Darrington Ranger District and Green Trails: Nos. 77 Oso,
78 Darrington

A small shallow lake, a gushing waterfall, and rugged cliffs in the head-waters of an unnamed tributary of Deer Creek set below 5274-foot Round Mountain. A great destination.

Oh! But wait a minute! Before putting the kids in the car for a fun day in the mountains, there are a few problems. First, the access road has water ditches passable to only those family cars with high clearance. The first mile of walking is on a decommissioned road with numerous

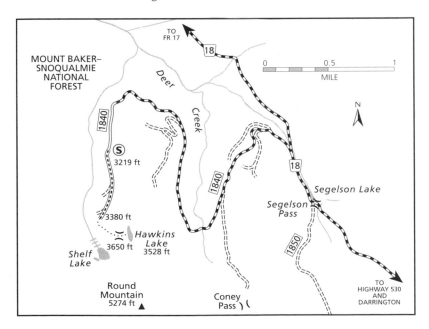

Hawkins Lake

water ditches and knee-deep brush. The last third mile is a boot-beaten path through a brush-covered clearcut. Sounds terrible—and it is—but the rewards are worth every scratch and aching muscle.

Driving directions: Drive State Highway 530 from I-5 toward Darrington. Near milepost 44, go left on Swede Heaven Road. At about 1.5 miles, go right on Forest Road 18 and start climbing to great views of Whitehorse Mountain. At 12.5 miles, go left on Road 1840 (here come the water ditches). At 3.3 miles, reach the end of the drivable road, elevation 3219 feet.

If it were not for the brush and numerous water ditches, the first mile of abandoned road would be easy. The abandoned road ends in a large cleared area with a view of a 250-foot-high cascading waterfall below Shelf Lake, high on Round Mountain. The view doesn't get any better. So get out the crackers and peanut butter and forget the lake.

For those who must see the other side of the mountain, find an obscure boot path plowing its way through heavy brush of an old clearcut, contouring up the hillside into old growth. Now comes the tricky part. While walking is easier in the timber, the path becomes faint and easy to lose. Note very carefully landmarks such as trees, logs, and stumps, as it is absolutely essential to find the exact trail on the way back. The route crosses a ridge and drops 125 feet to the lakeshore.

By Ira Spring

15 ROAD 2703 CIRCLE PEAK

Road status: Open to ORVs
Round trip: 3 miles
High point: 4500 feet
Elevation gain: 600 feet

Maps: Darrington Ranger District and Green Trails: Nos. 79
Snowking Mtn., 111 Sloan Peak

This is dramatic forested country that is easily accessible for the casual visitor. Roads open to beautiful mountain valleys and forested hillsides. The valley drive offers remote wild and scenic river encounters, views of streams and forested mountainsides. Today, the road is drivable to the

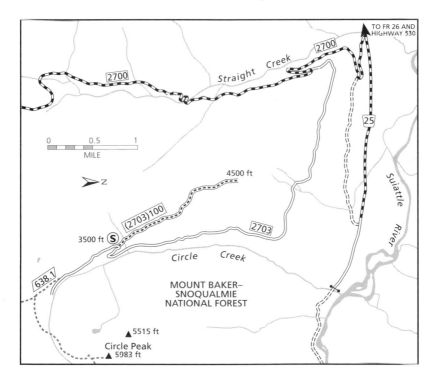

View from Road 2703-100 (photo by Jan Klippert)

end and probably it is more appropriate for mountain bikes than it is for hikers. New forests are masking scars of former clearcut areas. The roadbed is a typical Forest Service road that has not seen recent maintenance. There are ruts and spots where even a four-wheel-drive vehicle would want to slow down. It is a long drive to achieve adequate elevation for views of distant mountain ranges.

Driving directions: From SR 530, half way between Darrington and Rockport on the east side of the Sauk River crossing, the Suiattle River Road, FS Road 26, goes easterly to parallel the Suiattle River. It continues, taking you deep into the rugged mountains of the Cascade Range. At about 10 miles from SR 530, turn right on FS Road 25, crossing the Suiattle River in about 3 miles. Go right on FS Road 2700 and drive 4 miles to FS Road 2703. (As of August 2000, a major washout of FS Road 2700, 3 miles from the junction with FS Road 2703, does not allow a drivable connection with the White Chuck Road, FS Road 23.)

On FS Road 2703, 5.3 miles from FS Road 27, there is a fork in the road offering choices. At the end of the 1.5-mile, left-hand fork is Trail 638.1, leading to the top of Circle Peak, elevation 5983 feet. The right-hand road is scheduled to be decommissioned. For a walk, park at the fork, elevation 3500 feet. On foot go right 1½ miles to the end, at 4000 feet in elevation, for views of Circle Creek Valley and Circle Peak.

At the higher elevations FS Road 2703 is built on a steep hillside and offers the visitor excellent mountain views. Because of its relative remoteness, it offers escape for bikers and hikers seeking solitude and mountain vistas.

By Jan Klippert

16 ROAD 25
THE EXPLORERS TRAIL

Road status: Closed
Round trip: 1 to 14 miles
High point: 1800 feet
Elevation gain: 750 feet

Maps: Darrington Ranger District; Green Trails: Nos. 79
Snowking Mtn., 111 Sloan Peak, 80 Cascade Pass, and 112
Glacier Peak

An extraordinary and versatile trail indeed. There is plenty of road, good for biking as well as hiking. You also have the option of two sideroads that lead you off into different realms. A lot of folks just come to see the beautiful Gibson Falls, just a half mile in from the start of the trail. The falls is a trademark of this road/trail, in that most visitors find special satisfaction that they took the trouble to overcome some barriers to get to the falls, thus feeling worthy of respect as explorers. But many of these would-be explorers are unaware of the secrets to be found up the road. If only they went farther and kept their eyes open!

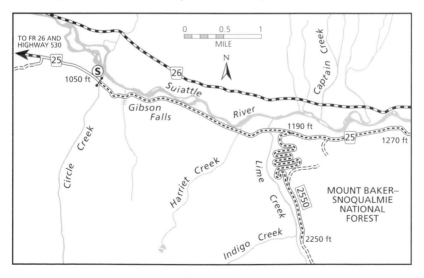

Driving directions: Take the Silvana/Arlington exit off I-5 onto Highway 530 East. Go 33 miles to Darrington. At the stop sign take a left. (Nice view of White Horse Mountain, huh? The last public bathroom that you're going to find on this stretch of road is the one at the gas station.) Follow the road 7 miles and, just after crossing the Sauk River, take a right onto the Suiattle River Road (FS Road 25). Ten miles later take a left over the Suiattle River (just after you cross the Suiattle River, look to your left for one of those beautiful roadside ponds) and follow the road to where it ends, 6 miles later at Circle Creek.

⛰

If you come early in the season, Circle Creek is likely to be raging. This also means that Gibson Falls is raging in its splendor, too. To safely get across, go upstream a couple hundred feet to a 4-foot-diameter hemlock growing on its side across the creek. I have easily carried my bike across it several times. If you come in late July, the creek should not be much more than ankle deep.

The road gradually climbs for a little less than a half mile to your next stream crossing, and Gibson Falls is upstream from there. The falls form a broad veil of water from three rivulets. It is pretty, but the canyon is cooled by the water vapor. I don't know why everyone wants to know, but there is no pool at the base of the falls.

Farther up the road, at the next crossing, follow the stream up to another falls, not quite as big as Gibson Falls but just as pretty. You'll want to step carefully up along the streambed; it would be a shame to damage the luscious emerald velvet moss banks. The streambed sparkles with silvery speckled rocks. I have a hard time resisting taking them home.

Just a little past Lime Creek, look up to your right and you should spot a warming shed a hundred feet up from the trail. When I first came across the shed, I thought it might be someone's home, so I left a note apologizing for any intrusion. When I came back a month later, the note was still there. It is pretty cool, stocked with a metal box, chair, and some early lithographs of the area. Another hundred feet up the hill from the shed is a nice rock cliff that looks like it may make for some interesting climbing.

The road starts to drop, and in another couple thousand feet you'll find yourself along the Suiattle River. The Suiattle, fed by Glacier Peak, seems to be raging at any time of the year. I've been told that at one time this river was good for steelhead, but not any more. You will get some good views of Green Mountain and its famous meadows.

The road runs along the Suiattle for 1300 feet and then goes uphill again, and you really don't see the river again. In a couple miles you come to a concrete bridge over Meadow Creek. Go just a little farther and take a right up a short road to a big clearing. The ground is level, smooth, and covered with soft grass. The creek is only a couple hundred feet a way. This is the perfect camp if you are not in any hurry.

Not too much farther up the road is the first sideroad. A mile and a half later is the second sideroad. You can still see some of the old road signs, but you really have to look for them, hidden in the overgrowth. The undergrowth on the road gets thick in places after the first fork.

On the first sideroad, I had a dream of taking it up to where I could bushwhack my way to Indigo Lake. The road rises steeply, with four or five switchbacks. Here you will get some stunning views of Green Mountain. In a shaded area, I came across beautiful patches of babies' breath in bloom. As the road travels along midway up the side of Lime Ridge, Meadow Mountain comes into view, with a brief glimpse of Glacier Peak.

Suiattle River (photo by Tom Karchesy)

Bunchberry

There are several beautiful areas to rest, with marmots and chipmunks coming out to greet you. The valley has its special solitude, with the noise of the river below. At points you can see Indigo Creek, across the valley.

The good road ends with three big rocks. I carried my bike past the rocks, and had to ditch it. Actually, the first thing I came across was three piles of bear scat. One looked pretty fresh, but I never saw any other signs of bear. The road had been plowed for a thousand feet and is now thick with mature saplings, but it is still hikable. Several areas past the closure have slid, but eventually you get to where the bridge across Meadow Creek used to be. Even late in the season the creek is impassable. I backtracked a few hundred feet, went down the hill to the creek, and found a fallen tree to cross on. Back up the other side, the road wasn't much better, but it still carried on to Indigo Creek. It is a strenuous climb up the hill to Indigo Lake.

Back down at the fork, it is another mile and half to the next sideroad. There is no elevation gain along the main road. Midway to the next fork, you pass through what looks like an old quarry. Here you can get a glimpse of some of the larger peaks in the area. I could hear the river nearby but I never really saw it again. I started up the second sideroad, which runs along the other side of Lime Ridge. It eventually stops at a steep impasse.

This road has a lot to offer; the flora and fauna, the artifacts—there are just a lot of hidden secrets to be discovered. I wish I had more time to explore at the farther reaches of the road. This also seems like a good place to visit in the winter, when snow is on the ground. The trees have a special beauty that would stand out against a snowy backdrop. It would definitely take a few seasons for one to truly explore this trail.

By Tom Karchesy

17 Road 2435-020
White Chuck Mountain

Road status: Open
Round trip: 2 miles to first flower meadow
High point: 5280 feet
Elevation gain: 400 feet

Maps: Darrington Ranger District and Green Trails: No. 111
Sloane Peak

The scenery is outstanding. The road is steep, but very drivable, to within 200 feet of its end, so this trip does not technically qualify as a road-to-trail. Still, the spectacular scenery from the boot-beaten climbers' path is too special to leave out.

Driving directions: From I-5, drive through Arlington to the four-way stop in Darrington. Go left 0.2 mile, then right 2.1 miles on Sauk Prairie Road, and then go right on Forest Road 24 for another 8 miles to a major junction. Go left on Road 2430 (not signed at time of research) for 0.5 mile, then right on Road 2435 (not signed). As the road climbs, panoramic

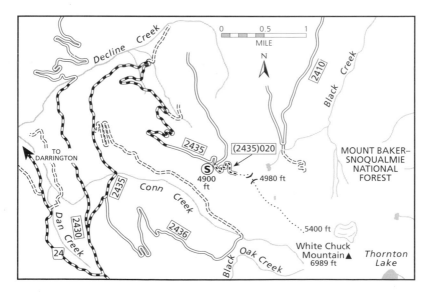

Mount Pugh, Mount Sloan, and the cloudy Sauk River valley from the side of White Chuck Mountain

views open. Whitehorse, Three Fingers, Forgotten, Sloan, Monte Cristo Peaks, Pugh, and the Rocky tower of White Chuck. At 5.5 miles from Road 24, go right (straight ahead) on Road 2435-020 (not signed) for another 0.5 mile to a large parking area, elevation 4900 feet.

▲

Many people will be satisfied just to stare at the view from their car window. Maybe it is best, for the climbers' path is rugged and very easy to lose.

For those who must see for themselves, walk to the road-end and find the boot-beaten path contouring steeply up an old clearcut. Much of the way the path is covered with brush, at times letting your feet feel the trail that you cannot see. Reaching virgin timber the brush is gone, but a massive blowdown must be crossed. First, though, cross a small meadow to its end for a great view of White Chuck Mountain.

Beyond the blowdown, the path is much easier as it follows the ups and downs of a narrow ridge. In about 1 mile we stopped in a small flower-covered meadow, elevation 5300 feet. Above were the boxlike faces of 6989-foot White Chuck Mountain. At our feet on this August day were phlox, lupine, paintbrush, penstemon, blue harebells, red heather, bistort, valerian, and three little glacier lilies.

We met four hikers who told us they had gone another ½ mile across a large, steep rockslide to camp at a tiny tarn with great views.

By Ira Spring

18 ROAD 2660
TENAS CREEK

Road status: Open to four-wheel drive; no gate—not drivable
Round trip: 4½ miles
High point: 4490 feet
Elevation gain: 1450 feet

Maps: Darrington Ranger District and Green Trails: No. 79
Snowking Mtn.

An overgrown Forest Service road, brushy becoming open. Tenas Creek draws its origin from the slopes of Hurricane Peak and Huckleberry Mountain, a valley adjacent to the Glacier Peak Wilderness. FS Road 2660 provides access deep into the valley and eventually leads hikers high onto an open mountainside and an abandoned road well worth taking.

Driving directions: Midway between Darrington and Rockport, SR 530 crosses the Sauk River. FS Road 26 intersects on the east side of the bridge. FS Road 26 then heads southerly and follows the Suiattle River deep into the Cascade Range. About 8.3 miles from the junction of SR 530

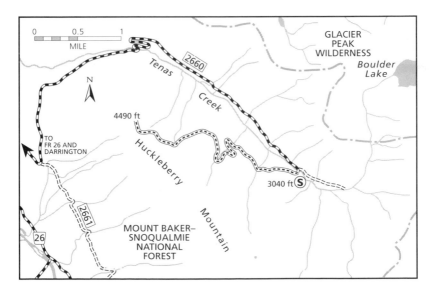

Cascade Mountain from the end of abandoned Road 2660 (photo by Jan Klippert)

and FS Road 26 is the connection with FS Road 2660, a gravel road that leads into the Tenas Creek valley. The road goes through lush forests, meadows, and a clearcut, with great views of the valley and surrounding mountain range.

Drive 7.5 miles on FS Road 2660. Near the end of the road is a large clearing. Nearby, Tenas Creek provides a good water supply. Other camping opportunities are numerous in the broad valley and there are several clearings along the road that provide adequate tenting sites.

Cross the creek and park, elevation 3040 feet. Don't try to drive farther.

The deteriorating roadbed goes up a steep incline to the left. Find the abandoned road and start hiking.

The first 0.4 mile of the unmaintained road is overgrown with alder. The tread is obvious and easy to follow. Soon the road opens to great views of the high ridges of Hurricane Peak and Huckleberry Mountain. The old road is in good shape for hikers and has great potential for mountain bikers.

The road continues steadily upward to 4490 feet. There are great views to the north of the Cascade Range and east to Illabot Peaks and Mount Chayal.

By Jan Klippert

19 ROAD 4110-024
GREEN MOUNTAIN

Road status: Closed
Round trip: 4¼ miles
High point: 3810 feet
Elevation gain: 900 feet

Maps: Darrington Ranger District and Green Trails No. 109
Granite Falls

Wow*eee*, what a view! Pilchuck, Three Fingers, Bigbear, and a bunch of other peaks. Before we could figure out what was what, clouds moved in and we were lucky to see our feet.

Driving directions: From the center of Granite Falls, drive the Mountain Loop Highway 7 miles toward Verlot and go left on Forest Road 41. Pass two driveways on the right and stay on the paved road signed No. 41. This is the last road sign on this road. The Forest Service his given up replacing them for target practice.

At 1.7 miles from the Mountain Loop Highway the pavement ends.

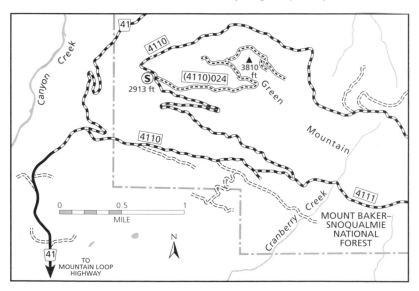

71

Three Fingers from Green Mountain

Go right on Road 4110 (no sign), go 1.8 miles to a major junction, then turn left (still on Road 4110) and drive another 2.3 miles, to a firmly blocked sideroad on the right, 5.9 miles from the Mountain Loop Highway, elevation 2913 feet.

The way starts with two humongous deep tank traps (trenches big enough to stop army tanks—or ORVs), riddled with broken glass and empty shotgun shells. If the pits are too difficult, bushwhack around them on the uphill side. There are a lot more water trenches, but none as bad as these two. In a long ¼ mile is a great view of Mount Pilchuck and out over the lowlands of Puget Sound. At about 1¼ miles, at an ancient rockslide, the road/trail turns left, climbing steadily and circling Green Mountain. If there were more deep water trenches on the north side of the mountain, we couldn't tell, for on the Memorial Day weekend we hiked the final, long ½ mile to the top, the road was covered with three feet of snow. The top had been leveled off and the ground was bare, a great place for a peanut butter sandwich. Obviously the views must be terrific in all directions, but none are guaranteed, for we had only a momentary view before we were engulfed in clouds.

The flat top would make a great campsite, to see the sunset and sunrise and lights in the lowlands, but the only water available would be snow, and that should be gone by mid-June.

By Ira Spring

20 Road 4111
Canyon Lake

Road status: Closed
Round trip: 5 miles
High point: 2959 feet
Elevation gain: Very little

Maps: Darrington Ranger District and Green Trails: Nos. 109
Granite Falls, 110 Silverton

What an easy, pleasant day hike or bike trip to a pretty backcountry lake.
Take the whole family.

Driving directions: From Granite Falls, drive east on the Mountain
Loop Highway 7 miles and turn left (north) on FR 41. This is the road to
Three Fingers and is directly opposite the Robe Canyon trailhead marker.
After turning north, immediately turn right (east) and proceed 1.7 miles on
FR 41 to the end of the pavement. Turn right and go east on FR 4110. At 3.4
miles, FR 4110 switches back to the left, but you continue straight on FR
4111 for 4 more miles. Park the family car where Turlo Creek crosses FR

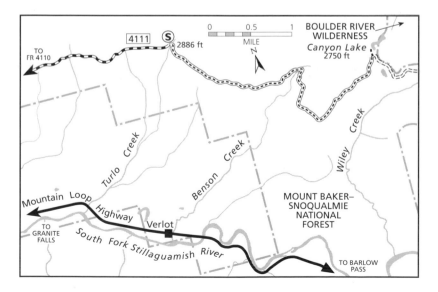

Canyon Lake (photo by John Howell)

4111, or, if you're in a four-wheel-drive vehicle, go on to the barricade, 7.4 miles from the Mountain Loop Highway exit, elevation 2886 feet.

▲▲

Walk or bike beyond the barricade on a level, solid roadbed. Within 0.7 mile, you'll see a small waterfall on your left, and later cross four small creeks. The fourth creek has an 18-foot-long footbridge that yearns for repair, but is safe. You will see foxglove, daisies, blackberries, creeping raspberries, shrubby cinquefoil, salmonberry, goats beard, and many other mountain flowers. In 2 miles is a fork. The main road goes straight and dead-ends in trees, with no views. Take the road angling to the right, which descends gradually for 0.3 mile. The trailhead to Canyon Lake is on the left, at the bottom of the hill, where the road turns right. Walk 0.2 mile up the trail to Canyon Lake, which is on your right. The trail takes you directly to the lakeshore, elevation 2750 feet.

It's a nice place for a picnic lunch. This 5-acre lake warms up enough for swimming, and reportedly has fish in it. There are three primitive tent sites near the lake. Previously, the trail continued along the west side of the lake heading north. This part of the trail is overgrown and is no longer noticeable.

By John Howell

21 ROAD 4039
SOLITUDE

A FEW HOURS OF SOLITUDE, VIEWS, AND SUNSHINE

Road status: Closed
Round trip: 4 miles
High point: 3300 feet
Elevation gain: 1256 feet

Maps: Darrington Ranger District and Green Trails: No. 110
Silverton

The day was too beautiful to stay home, but in May there was too much snow in the high country to go very far. As a compromise, Pat and I headed for Barlow Pass for an easy hike to Monte Cristo, or if there was too much snow, a simple walk to the Ice Caves below Big Four.

The drive was beautiful in Robe Valley and the glistening snow made Pilchuck look like a mighty mountain. The Stillaguamish was running high, as were our expectations. However, just beyond Silverton, everything came to a screeching halt! The road was blocked with heavy

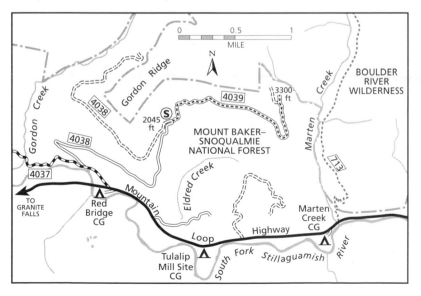

A small waterfall beside abandoned Road 4039

equipment replacing a bridge. (Why wasn't there a sign back at Granite Falls stating that, due to road construction, the road would be closed at Silverton until late May?)

Disgusted, we turned around and headed for snowcovered Lake 22. However, at 0.2 mile upriver from Red Bridge, we went exploring the River Road, located on the north side of the river.

Driving directions: To reach Red Bridge and the beginning of the walk, drive the Mountain Loop Highway (Highway 20) from Granite Falls. At some 11 miles, pass the Verlot Visitors Center, and go another 7 miles to Red Bridge. Just 0.2 mile beyond the bridge, turn left on a dirt road, No. 4037 signed River Road. In a short 0.3 mile, turn right on Forest Road 4038 and drive another 1.9 miles, to its end at a Y, where the road was blocked by a humungous water ditch, elevation 2046 feet. Time to walk.

▲▲

We walked the left-hand road for 2 miles. There were a lot of shot-up bottles and shotgun shells, but there were no views. However, there was pile after pile of bear droppings, fifteen or twenty, some fresh, a few from the previous year.

Next, we took the right-hand road, No. 4039. It was a good choice. The first ditch showed signs of some four-wheel drive climbing over the top, into the hole, and out again. A hundred feet farther were tracks into and out of another deep ditch. At the third ditch only a motorcycle track was visible, and by the fourth ditch only a few boot prints. There were twenty-seven of those deep ditches in the 1½ miles to the first the opening in the trees at 2700 feet. The view was good and we could have stopped here, but there is the urge to see what the bear saw on the other side of the mountain. We forgot to count the ditches in the next ½ mile to the road's end on top of a clearcut, at 3300 feet on Gordon Ridge overlooking Marten Creek Valley, right on the edge of the Boulder River Wilderness. Time for the peanut butter and Wheat Thins and a lazy hour looking down to the river and out to Mallardy Ridge.

A 2-mile road walk may not seem like much, but the deep ditches and almost 1256 feet in elevation gain was a good challenge after a winter's hibernation.

By Ira Spring

22 ROAD 4030-040
MALLARDY RIDGE

Road status: Open to four-wheel drive
Round trip: 2 miles
High point: 3000 feet
Elevation gain: 260 feet

Maps: Darrington Ranger District and Green Trails: No. 110 Silverton

There wasn't a cloud in the sky this Saturday afternoon. We drove the Mountain Loop Highway from Granite Falls to Verlot. The parking lot at the Lake 22 trailhead was jammed, twenty cars were at the Mount Dickerman trailhead, and there were thirty at Barlow Point. It is great to have everyone out in the mountains, but today there were too many people. We headed up Road 4030 to the Walt Bailey trail, but got stopped by a snowbank at about 3500 feet. On the way back we spotted this interesting sideroad, No. 4030-040 (not signed).

This proved to be a short, interesting walk between second growth and a virgin forest and best of all we had solitude. (The views were good, but we had passed a better view at 3400 feet.) The road is passable to a jeep and maybe to anyone with a scratched-up, high-clearance car.

Gordon Ridge from Mallardy Ridge

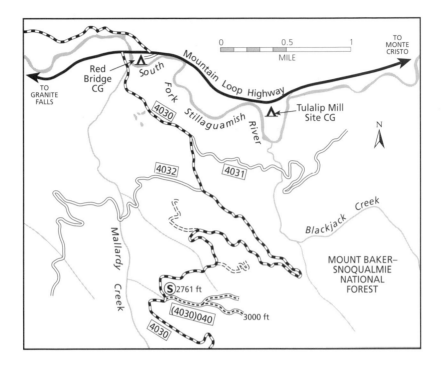

Driving directions: Drive the Mountain Loop Highway from Granite Falls to 6.9 miles past Verlot. Just short of the Red Bridge, turn right on Road 4030. At 1.3 miles, reach the end of the pavement at a Y; stay left (straight ahead). At 4.4 miles from the Mountain Loop Highway, find Road 4030-040 (not signed) climbing steeply to the left. Best to park here, elevation 2761 feet.

Drive this road if you can, but why? If it is only a view that is wanted, you could continue driving up Road 4030 another ½ mile for a wider and higher sweep—but, of course, that would miss the whole point of walking. Road 4030-040 is not maintained and alders are encroaching. The tread is easy to walk and the water dips are mild.

In about 1 mile reach a large landing with huge piles of rotting wood. From here the rugged east wall of Mount Pilchuck can be seen, a small portion of Three Fingers sticking above the horizon, Mount Stillaguamish to the right, and directly across the valley is Gordon Ridge, with road-to-trail No. 4039 (Hike 21) traversing its side.

By Ira Spring

23 ROAD 4054
DEVILS RIDGE

Road status: Closed
Round trip: 4 miles
High point: 2500 feet
Elevation gain: 500 feet

Maps: Darrington Ranger District and Green Trails: No. 110
Silverton

This is a nice, easy day hike close to the Mountain Loop Highway, with views and a waterfall below Devils Peak.

Driving directions: From Granite Falls, drive east on the Mountain Loop Highway 23.8 miles to FR 4052. Turn left and drive north on FR 4052 for 1 mile. Here the road curves left. Park on the right at the junction with abandoned FR 4054, elevation 1968 feet.

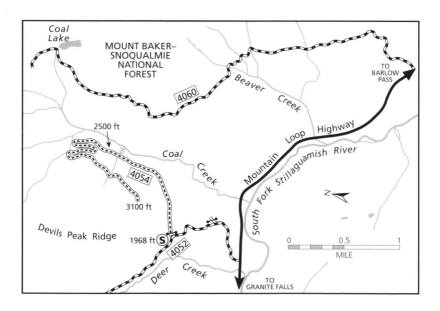

Big Four Mountain and the Stillaguamish River valley, seen from abandoned Road 5054

Hike up the old road among columbine, goats beard, fireweed, raspberries, and more. At 1 mile there is a gorgeous view of Big Four Mountain, Vesper Peak, Sperry Peak, and Lewis Peak to the south. At 2 miles there is a 12-foot-wide wooden bridge crossing a creek. Directly to the left is a beautiful waterfall, with its creek running under the bridge. The easy hike to the mountain view and waterfall make this hike worthwhile for families and is a pleasant getaway. It is a gentle uphill hike, with fifty-one dirt mound/ditch barriers across the trail in the first 2 miles. The barriers are easy enough for hikers but render the trail usable for hikers only.

There is no incentive to go farther. At 3 miles the trail becomes overgrown with alder, devils club, and berry bushes. At this point, hiking is difficult and there are no more views to enjoy.

By John Howell

24 COUNTY ROAD
MONTE CRISTO TOWN

Road status: Gated
Round trip: 8 miles
High point: 2756 feet
Elevation gain: 400 feet

Maps: Darrington Ranger District and Green Trails: Nos. 143 Monte Cristo, 111 Sloan Peak

It was the first clear day in several weeks, and it came on a weekend. The hike to Monte Cristo is popular, so, to avoid the mob, we reached Barlow Pass at 8:00 A.M. and still counted ten cars that had arrived before us.

Driving directions: From Granite Falls, drive the Mountain Loop Highway (Highway 20) some 30 miles to Barlow Pass, elevation 2361 feet.

This is a wonderful trip any time of the year, and especially in June when the pussy willows and trillium are blooming and the mountains

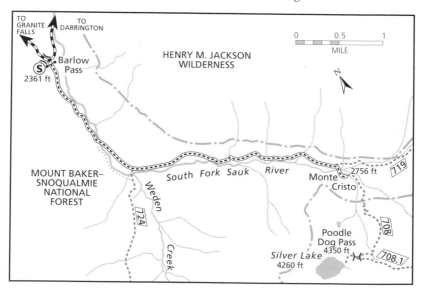

View from the Monte Cristo road

are plastered with snow. In June there will be patches of snow to cross.

We remember driving this road in 1948, when the remains of an old railroad snow shed was still lying beside the road, and a series of campgrounds lined the way. There were Twin Bridges, Weldon House, Hops Hill, Silvertip, Sauk River, and Monte Cristo Campgrounds. Since our first trip some of the buildings have disappeared, but the ghost town that is left has history written all over it.

On December 26, 1986, floodwater took out a bridge, sections of the road, and the campgrounds. Rather than repair the road, the county gated it at Barlow Pass, changing a dusty road to a delightful hike and bicycle trail. It may seem strange, but it is more fun now than when we drove it. Silver Lake and Glacier Basin are a bit longer but can still be hiked in a day.

The parking lot at Barlow Pass must have been filling up fast, as hikers and bicycles were soon passing us. However, it was nothing compared to the numbers that passed us as we headed back to the car. One family, on bicycles, had two young kids on bicycles with training wheels. The youngest was more interested in climbing logs beside the road than riding. Except for several rude bicyclists coming from behind, who whizzed by only inches away without warning, hikers and bicycles did fine together.

While the county has abandoned the road, private property owners have made it a four-wheel-drive route, and a number of people have gate keys, so the trip is not entirely car-free.

By Ira Spring

25 ROAD 4096
CHOCWICH CREEK FALLS

Road status: Closed

CHOCWICH CREEK FALLS
Round trip: 4¼ miles
High point: 2250 feet
Elevation gain: 450 feet

ELLIOTT CREEK TO BEDAL CREEK
Round trip: 7 miles
High point: 2700 feet
Elevation gain: 900 feet

Maps: Darrington Ranger District and Green Trails: No. 111 Sloan Peak

This is a nice, easy trail for hiking or biking to a lovely waterfall.

Driving directions: To get to Elliott Creek, drive north on the Mountain Loop Highway (Highway 20) 3.6 miles from Barlow Pass to FR 4080. Turn right (east) on FR 4080 and go 0.8 mile to the Goat Lake trailhead, elevation 1880 feet.

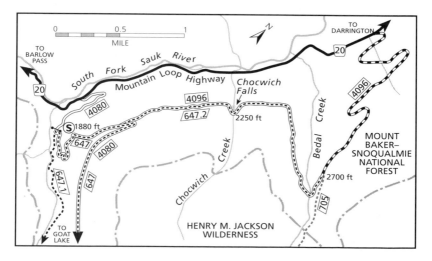

Bike or hike 1.1 miles up the Goat Lake Trail to a trail junction. Right (straight ahead) is the hiker-only trail to Goat Lake. For Chocwich Creek Falls, bikers and hikers angle to the left as the trail narrows. This is the former FR 4096. Take this trail another mile north to Chocwich Creek and an impressive waterfall.

To go farther, large rocks provide an easy ford of Chocwich Creek. Travel another 1.4 miles through forest to Bedal Creek. There is one clearing giving a mountain and valley view to the north, toward Darrington.

Crossing Bedal Creek with or without a bike is doable, but not recommended. In a few minutes, you are at the steep FR 4096, featuring washouts and loose gravel. This road is unfriendly to bikes and family cars, but okay for high-clearance, four-wheel-drives other than ORVs. I recommend going up Elliot Creek to the waterfall at Chocwich Creek (4.2 miles round trip). If you like, continue another 1.4 miles through pleasant forest on good trail except for a few drainage dips across the trail. This makes a nice 7-mile round trip to Bedal Creek.

By John Howell

Chocwich Creek Falls (photo by John Howell)

26 ROAD 49
PRIDE BASIN VIEW

Road status: Proposed to be closed
Round trip: 3 miles
High point: 5000 feet
Elevation gain: 2000 feet

Maps: Darrington Ranger District and Green Trails: No. 111
Sloan Peak

This trip offers great views of the small glaciers in Pride Basin.

Driving directions: On the Mountain Loop Highway (Highway 20), drive 7 miles north from Barlow Pass, or 16 miles south from Darrington, to FR 49. Go east on FR 49 for 15.3 miles to its end. At 13.3 miles, there is a lovely campsite along Bowser Creek where it crosses the road.

At road's end, there is a gorgeous view of Sloan Peak (7835 feet in elevation). Walking beyond the dirt barrier at road's end, the old road continues

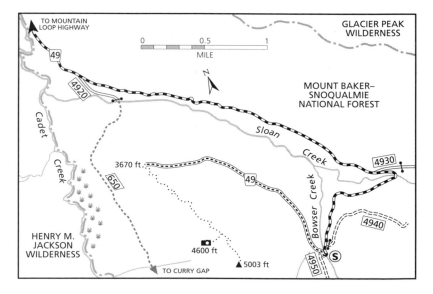

Sloan Peak from the end of the abandoned road (photo by John Howell)

for a short distance. A narrow, unmaintained trail can be seen to the left. It goes up moderately for 1.5 miles, seemingly to nowhere. Routefinding skills are useful here, as the route seems to disappear and reappear several times. The trail meanders up through forest with no views until near the top. If you go to the right (west) side of this ridge and look west, there is a spectacular, knockout view of Sloan Peak to the north and Cadet, Monte Cristo, and Kyes Peaks side by side to the south. There is no sidetrail to this spot and it isn't easy to find, but what a spectacular place to have lunch in solitude on a sunny day!

By John Howell

27 ROAD 2060
CLEAR CREEK VALLEY

Road status: Proposed to be closed

TO ROAD-END
Round trip: 8½ miles
High point: 2800 feet
Elevation gain: 1200 feet

TO DEER CREEK PASS
Round trip: 10½ miles
High point: 3400 feet
Elevation gain: 1600 feet

Maps: Darrington Ranger District map and Green Trails: No. 110 Silverton

The Clear Creek Valley, just outside Darrington, is a small, relatively lonely watershed rimmed by steep cliffs with interesting, exposed rock faces. The logging and mining activity that the roads served was long enough ago that many of the most obvious scars have healed, and there is a healthy second-growth forest with impressive relict old-growth patches here and there.

Driving directions: To get to the road's beginning, drive 3 miles on the Mountain Loop Highway (Highway 20) from Darrington, then bear left on the obvious FS Road 2060, just across from the Clear Creek Campground. Go 5.3 miles, to a fork. For road/trail No. 2060 park here, on the left, elevation 1600 feet. At this writing the road is still open to traffic, but from the looks of the road it sees very little use, especially the last mile or so.

▲▲

Though it is close to Darrington and the Mountain Loop Highway, there are relatively few traces of visitors on this road, and the day I was there I saw not a soul the whole day, though it was a sunny summer Sunday.

Road 2060 takes the high route up the Clear Creek valley, offering a more rewarding walk than the low road, No. 2065 (Hike 28), which runs parallel along the valley floor.

I walked up Road 2060 on a hot day, working up enough of a sweat on the exposed sections that I appreciated the shade that covers about half the 4-mile route. The road offers a pleasant stroll up the peaceful mountain valley, with views at the beginning and end. The road/trail gains 1500 feet in even, gradual stages, ending at the trailhead for Deer Creek Pass.

The route starts on a sturdy concrete bridge over Clear Creek, which offers beaches and excellent nearby campsites for those interested in relaxing by a shady river. Two large campsites, one in use on the day I scouted the trail, are well back from the road and private from each other. Trails connect these sites to the water. Shortly past the campsites, the forest road breaks into the open, and for the next half mile or so, views are continuous as the road contours its way up the valley wall, hundreds of feet above Clear Creek and its surrounding forest. At 0.6 mile is an exposed, waterless campsite with excellent views up the valley to the snow-capped face of Liberty Mountain. Campers might be advised to wait until the road is actually closed to traffic to camp at this particular

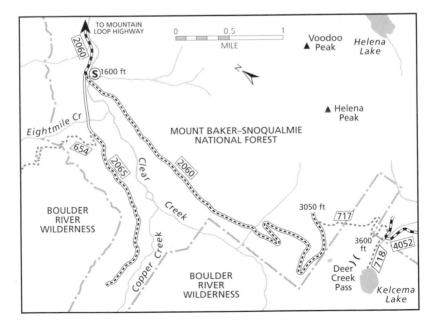

Three Fingers from Road 2060 (photo by Gary Faigin)

spot, as it is uncomfortably close to the roadbed, should anyone choose to drive by.

At 1½ miles, the road enters the forest, never so far from the valley wall that views cannot be glimpsed through the trees, but offering relief from the sun on a hot day. Water is plentiful, but often difficult to reach as streams rush beneath the road in culverts well below the built-up road level.

At 3½ miles, views open up for good, with Three Fingers and Whitehorse gradually emerging from behind nearby ridges, and Bear and Liberty Mountains to the left. This is a good spot for lunch, sitting with one's legs at road's edge. There is a campsite at the road-end, with a plentiful source of water adjacent. Attentive hikers will note the two cairns marking the Deer Creek Pass trailhead, less than a mile from Kelcema Lake by a not-terribly-steep trail.

By Gary Faigin

28 ROAD 2065
COPPER CREEK VALLEY

Road status: Proposed to be closed
Round trip: 6 miles
High point: 2000 feet
Elevation gain: 300 feet

Maps: Darrington Ranger District and Green Trails: No. 110
Silverton

I walked up Road 2065 on a cloudless day in July, when snow still lingered on many of the visible peaks above tree line, and the shade on the road was a blessing. The shade was also a problem—this particular road, hemmed in by mature second-growth forest, offers no real view for the several miles it takes to gain the end of the trail, although it is surrounded by beautiful ridges and peaks. The area does offer several attractions, however. It is low enough in elevation to be available in all but the snowiest months, and there are several campsites (one alongside a swimming hole) that do not show signs of much recent visitation. This small, quiet valley also ends in wilderness, to which this trail gives access.

Driving directions: To reach Road 2065, follow the Mountain Loop Highway 3 miles from Darrington. Bear right on the obvious Forest Service road (No. 2060) just across from the Clear Creek Campground. At 5.3 miles is the intersection with Road 2065; continue right another 0.7 mile. Park at the Squire Creek trailhead, at 6 miles, elevation 1700 feet.

The walking route up Road 2065 starts at the trailhead for the "back way" up to Squire Creek Pass, an unmaintained trail marked with an old hubcap on a tree stump. I would have missed it completely had there not been two cars parked there, presumably belonging to hikers headed up to the pass. Just beyond the trailhead for Squire Creek is a small Forest Service sign indicating that the road beyond, 2065, is slated for possible closure.

The route up 2065 is level and uneventful, mostly in deep woods, with the occasional peekaboo view of impressive nearby cliffs. The road is still in excellent condition, quite passable even in the family sedan. The road essentially follows Clear Creek for the first mile, winding up the Copper Creek valley floor until joining the creek at trail's end. Road 2060 (Hike 27) runs up the same valley, but it contours up the opposite valley wall, offering more expansive views.

At 1½ miles, there is an obvious spur road going off to the left. The spur road goes straight downhill ½ mile to a large campsite next to a beautiful stretch of Clear Creek. There are several short trails from the campsite to swimming holes in the creek, the biggest pool perhaps 4 feet deep.

Back on the main route, just past the spur, was a dusty car, packed with camping equipment and draped with two sleeping bags drying out in the sun. I never saw anyone on the trail, and given the limited options of places to go along this route, I was left wondering where the people had gone.

Past the spur, the forest opens up enough to allow more territorial views. There are two large campsites with well-constructed fire pits. Neither campsite has nearby water, but both have interesting vantage points looking toward massive exposed rock faces across the valley floor. The second campsite is located, not too appealingly, amidst the bleached debris of a former log staging area.

From this point the road deteriorates into a rough trail, plunging into deep woods and going over more rugged terrain, the trail easy enough

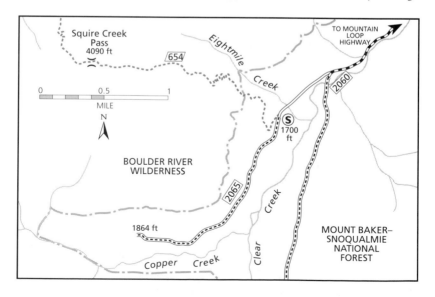

for a hiker, but steep and narrow enough in spots to challenge a trail biker. At some places the route is a bit difficult to follow, but enough travelers have beaten a path through the trees and brush to keep the way open. I was mystified to discover blue tape flagging along the trail, with notations such as "W/B lead-in ditch," as though a trail crew was about to come through for some routine maintenance. Who would be maintaining this trail, and why? My maps were no help here, as I could find no indication of where this unmarked, unmapped trail might go.

The sound of Copper Creek, unseen along most of the route, becomes louder and louder. The trail passes rusting debris of an old mining operation. Finally, at about 3 miles, the trail crosses boulders in a large dry streambed, then reaches the creek itself. The creek crossing looked to be the most intriguing part of the route. The creek itself is full of pools and cataracts, and at last one has a clear view of the

Copper Creek (photo by Gary Faigin)

snow-capped mountains, previously hidden by the forest. Just on the other side, the way seemed to break into the open, perhaps trending up the talus slope toward the cirque at the head of the valley. But other than a faded yellow tape waving from a tree just across the creek, probably put there by a rock climber, I could see no obvious route through the chest-high brush across the way, or beyond, up the open slope. Nor did I note a likely campsite on either side of the creek. As I was not prepared for the half-body soak a crossing of the creek would require, I opted, this time, to leave exploring the far bank for another day. One prepared for bushwhacking and backcountry travel, perhaps arriving when the creek was a bit lower, might well push on beyond this ford toward the beckoning ridge tops.

By Gary Faigin

29 ROAD 2087
FALLS CREEK

Road status: Open to four-wheel drive

TO FALLS CREEK BRIDGE
Round trip: 8 miles
High point: 1350 feet
Elevation gain: 310 feet

TO MOUNT PUGH VIEW
Round trip: 9½ miles
High point: 2900 feet
Elevation gain: 760 feet

Maps: Darrington Ranger District and Green Trails: No. 111 Sloan Peak

Walk within sight of the Sauk River and meandering Falls Creek to views.

Driving directions: Drive the Mountain Loop Highway 9 miles south from Darrington or 14.4 miles north from Barlow Pass and turn west on FR 2080. At 1.1 miles is the junction with FR 2081 and a sign indicating the Peek-a-boo Lake Trail is to the right. For Falls Creek, stay straight ahead for 2.4 miles. Park where Peek-a-boo Creek crosses FR 2080, elevation 1060

Salal near the Falls Creek bridge

feet. (High-clearance vehicles can drive on to the road-end.) Traffic is rare and walking is good. The road ends 2 miles from Peek-a-boo Creek at a dirt barricade near the Falls Creek bridge, elevation 1330 feet. (Old maps show Road 2080 followed Falls Creek up valley for several miles, then a trail continued to North Lake and Pass Lake. Logging obliterated the trail and floods and dense brush obliterated the road.)

On foot, cross pretty Falls Creek on an old moss-covered, wooden bridge where the road becomes Road 2087. This road is grown over with alder, devils club, and raspberry bushes in many spots. After hiking through brush for a few minutes it opens up in places for easy, gradual uphill hiking or biking. At 0.6 mile from the bridge, the old road is washed out in a gully and the view opens up to the east. There is a beautiful view of Mount Pugh, jutting up from behind a ridge, elevation 1800 feet.

Going on, the trail switches back to the right at 1.7 miles just before coming to a creek. I went 75 feet past the switchback and the trail disappears in a washout containing blowdowns. I did not find the trail beyond this point. I do not recommend going on unless you can find where the trail continues.

By John Howell

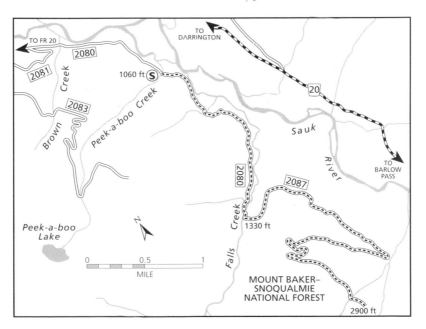

30 DNR ROAD
OLNEY CREEK ROAD

Road status: Closed
Round trip: 16½ miles
High point: 3640 feet
Elevation gain: 2900 feet

Maps: Skykomish Ranger District and Green Trails: No. 142
Index

Headed out Saturday morning to do the Olney Creek Road, up near Sultan Basin, for Ira's "roads to trails" project. Planned to start hiking about 10:30 A.M. and hoped to include a bushwhack to Lake Stickney as part of the package.

Driving directions: On US Highway 2, just east of Sultan, turn north on County Road 61, signed "Sultan Recreation Area," and drive some 12 miles to a few feet beyond the Olney Creek bridge. Find the abandoned road on the right, elevation 1679 feet.

Off to a bad start. First, I'm my usual half hour behind schedule. Then we ran into almost an extra hour of bumper-to-bumper traffic from Woodinville to Sultan. Everybody heading out to see the fall colors, I guess. Anyway, after Andy, our dog Ginger, and I finally started walking, just before noon, things got better and stayed better for quite awhile, although the day turned out to be unexpectedly hot. In 6 hours we did 11 miles and 2500 feet—plus another 2 miles and 500 feet after dark! Andy and Ginger actually took longer, but that's part of the "bad day," and we're not there yet.

The first 1½ miles of the ungated Olney Creek Road are 4-x-4 drivable, although the family car would quickly be swallowed in road-spanning puddles. It's pleasant walking in country that feels more like an Appalachian hollow than a typical Cascade valley, partly because of the high proportion of deciduous trees.

The next 4 miles are marred by eighty-eight trenches (I counted 'em on the way down, and probably missed some), plus about a mile of

DNR's complete road demolition, euphemistically called "restoring the natural slope," a process resulting in landscape indistinguishable from a strip mine. The walking is not so much fun.

Just over 4 miles in, we reached the logging landing where we hoped to turn off and bushwhack to Lake Stickney. Actually, I hoped we might find a way trail leading to it. On the map it's only ¼ mile from the road, but the route would almost certainly be at least half a mile.

However, the main road kept going, up and over the ridge to the east; down to and across the south fork of the South Fork Sultan River; and up to the top of another ridge with views into Kromona Basin and the rugged valley of the north fork of the South Fork, as well as Mount Stickney, Mount Pilchuck, and Spada Reservoir. This section of road was about 1¼ miles longer than what shows on the map, so by the time we stopped for lunch at road-end, about 3:30 P.M., it was obvious that we weren't going to Lake Stickney.

And that's too bad, because Lake Stickney is going to be an interesting destination for somebody. It's bigger than you'd expect, almost as long as Wallace Lake although not as wide, and dotted with little islands. Hidden in a trough west of the road, it is the source of Olney Creek and is deep in a stretch of old-growth forest. Fish have been reported, as has a way trail that only leads from the lake, not to it!

About the time we got back to the Lake Stickney turnoff, the bad part

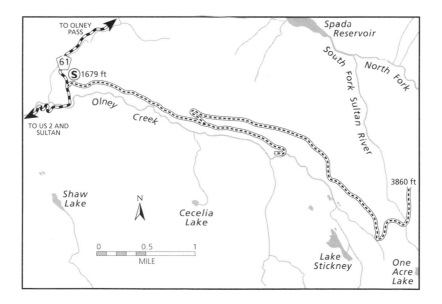

Spada Reservoir (photo by David Head)

of the day began. Ginger started slowing down, apparently done in by the geology. Most of the road is cut through an area of quartzite schist, rich in sharp flakes of mica, and the road is paved with the stuff. It began to get to her feet. Then, somewhere on the way down, she sliced one of her pads really badly—and at 5:15 P.M. she just stopped and lay down, and no amount of encouragement would get her started again.

There was really no question about what would happen next. Andy would not leave the dog (that's a given in our world). So I would leave the two of them and go for help. (One of the things I couldn't do was carry the dog. I tried, but Ginger weighs at least a hundred pounds.) At 5:30 P.M. I started down the trail, hoping that I would be able to get in touch with my son.

There are worse things than having an unofficial "search and rescue" unit in the family. My son Dave is a fireman, an EMT in training, a mountain climber—and he drives a big four-wheel-drive pickup. (He may also be this generation's Clark Kent.)

I covered the 2½ miles and thirty trenches back to the car in forty-five minutes. Jogging on the flat, half-blinded by the setting sun, I tripped and twisted an ankle and banged up one knee. Then twenty minutes in the car back to Sultan, and then fifteen frustrating minutes trying to make a phone call.

But Dave was home and things started looking brighter. He lives just east of Lake Stevens and it took him only thirty minutes to get his stuff together and get to me in Sultan. Another twenty minutes back to the Olney Creek Road and I parked my car and climbed into the truck. It took five minutes in the truck to do the mile and a half to the end of drivable road.

I gave him a thermos of hot coffee and some extra clothes to put in his pack and sent him on the road ahead of me. There was no way I could keep up with him, and the sooner someone got back to Andy the better. One mile, 500 feet, thirty trenches—it took him eighteen minutes. When I got there about ten minutes later, Andy had already had coffee and Dave had tried several different sling arrangements on Ginger, though so far without success.

Andy had been alone only three hours and had gotten on pretty well. The night was mercifully warm and she had a working flashlight and extra clothes if she needed them, although no extra food. She kept occupied bringing Ginger water from a nearby streamlet and trying to estimate how long it might take me to get back. Her spirits were probably saved when we arrived back about two hours faster than her "best" estimate.

Dave finally got a sling worked out, hoisted Ginger to his shoulders, and took off down the trail—just like that. He went all the way back down to the truck without stopping, 1 mile, thirty trenches, with a hundred-pound dog on his back, in less than fifteen minutes, most of the time without light(!). And Dave wasn't even breathing hard.

Needless to say, the rest of the day went better. We followed Dave back to Lake Stevens, where his wife had dinner waiting for us. After dinner it was flashlights again as we went outside to admire the pond that Dave had spent the last 3 days lining with twenty tons of rock.

And finally home to bed. A big improvement over what might have been the alternative.

By Dave Head

31 DNR ROAD
BLUE MOUNTAIN

Road status: Half the distance gated
Round trip: 3½ miles
High point: 2955 feet
Elevation gain: 950 feet

Maps: Skykomish Ranger District and Green Trails: No. 142
Index

Here's a quick hike to a splendid viewpoint, little visited and close to town. The distance to the viewpoint is about 1¾ mile, the elevation gain just a bit under 1000 feet. Bring your own water.

Driving directions: To reach the beginning of Blue Mountain Road, drive the Sultan Basin Road (Road 61) 13.5 miles from US Highway 2, starting just east of Sultan. A scant quarter mile before the registration station, find an obvious turnoff to the left and park, elevation 2034 feet.

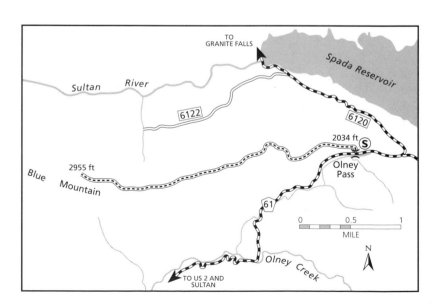

I walked up the road to Blue Mountain on a bright, near-freezing November day, the week before Thanksgiving. It had been a dry autumn with few storms, but there was still a dusting of snow at the trailhead, and lots of patches of ice. The road/trail starts just off Sultan Basin Road, a few hundred feet before the registration station at Olney Pass.

A sign announces the presence of a locked gate, but that is not encountered till the viewpoint, leaving the road open to vehicles at the time of research. I passed one truck on my way down, and there probably are regular wheeled visitors to the top during nicer weather.

The road, broad and easy to follow, starts very steeply up through

Abandoned Blue Mountain Road

Road-end on Blue Mountain (photo by Gary Faigin)

dry, pleasant woods. The dusting of snow at the turnoff turned to compact snow and ice by the top of the hill, about 1½ miles from the start, and I was watching my footing carefully on the way down.

The other thing that kept me a bit nervous on this chilly day, besides the slippery footing, was the repeated sound of gunfire. If I hadn't noticed several groups of target shooters on my way up the road, I might have wondered if a war had broken out. All afternoon the hills echoed with firing, sometimes far away, sometimes near. I heard several rounds of what must have been an automatic rifle of some sort, judging by the quick and continuous bursts of gunfire. I calculated my chances of taking a stray round as remote, thanks to my steeply upslope location. But all that noise made me nervous.

After about 50 minutes of steady walking, the road leveled out onto a broad turnaround, and suddenly a vast panorama opened up. The view was terrific, nearly 360 degrees, taking in everything from the town of Sultan and the Skykomish Valley to the southwest, to Mount Pilchuck and Puget Sound to the north, to various hills and ranges beyond the Sultan Basin to the east. There was a campsite in the middle of the turnaround, with a huge fire pit but absolutely no nearby water.

Just beyond this point is a securely closed gate, and the road continues on along the ridge top, encouraging further explorations. As for me, I beat out the fading light and carefully negotiated my way down the icy road, savoring the quiet that had descended on the woods as the marksmen took a break.

Here's an excellent trail opportunity—even better if a gate could be installed at the beginning of the road. It would be fun to camp at the viewpoint and not have to worry about wheeled visitors at all hours.

By Gary Faigin

32 DNR ROAD
KROMONA MINE

Road status: Gated
Round trip: 9 miles
High point: 2500 feet
Elevation gain: 600 feet

Maps: Skykomish Ranger District and Green Trails: No. 142
Index

On many hiking trails, the experience along the trail is incidental to getting to the destination—a view, a waterfall, a lake, a campsite. On the Kromona Mine Road, the experience on the trail is the whole point, since the route ends abruptly at a downed bridge with little of interest beyond.

Driving directions: To reach the Kromona Mine Road, turn left (north) on the Sultan Basin Road (Road 61) just east of the town of Sultan on US Highway 2. At 13.6 miles on the Sultan Basin Road there is a registration booth and a sign announcing the beginning of the Everett Watershed. Park

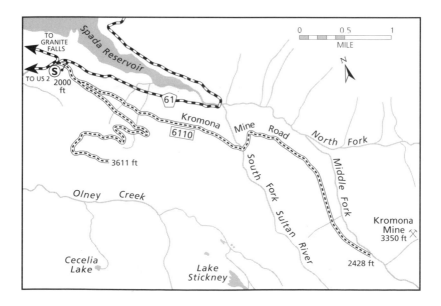

in the large turnoff just past the booth, where the road forks. Here you will find the gated Kromona Mine Road, elevation 2000 feet.

The 4½-mile route gains about 600 feet, and its elevation makes it a good bet for a shoulder season route when the high country is still white and inaccessible.

Go for the hike, not the destination, and you will be well rewarded. And if you're on a mountain bike, as I was, you may well find yourself adding this route to your short list of Best Mountain Bike Roads Close to Seattle. For the casual rider, this is an ideal jaunt on a scenic road, closed to traffic, with great views and an easy grade.

I traveled the Kromona Mine Road on a cool day in mid-August. Watching the hordes of recreational drivers on jeeps and motorcycles rushing past the trailhead on the Sultan Basin Road, I was grateful for the sturdy locked gate that kept this particular road vehicle-free. The steep initial hill just past the gate had me wondering if my bicycle legs were up for the ride, but very soon the road leveled out and stayed more or less level for the next 4½ miles.

The road surface is in excellent shape, providing few obstacles. It starts in a healthy second-growth forest, logged perhaps forty or fifty years ago. The way is rimmed with flowers, including daisies, foxglove, and paintbrush. Numerous streams rush underneath the road, full of water even after several weeks with no rain. The occasional pile of bear scat dotted the ground.

Views begin within the first mile, north to the Spada Reservoir, northeast to Greider Ridge, and east to the unnamed peaks of the Ragged Ridge. At 2½ miles, the road crosses a sturdy wooden bridge high over the gorge of a branch of the Sultan River. Pause and admire the exposed rock leading down to the stream. Wonder at the giant uprooted trees stacked upstream from the bridge, their roots destabilized by logging, road building, and washouts. Imagine continuing from this point if the bridge wasn't there—not an attractive possibility.

Past the bridge the views begin to widen as the road becomes a bit rougher. Now the mountains above the road's end appear to the south— the impressive steep rise of Mount Stickney, its walls still dotted with snow even this late in the summer. The view of the valley of the North Fork of the Sultan is even more impressive, the jagged profile of Ragged Ridge making the name seem appropriate. A look at the map reveals that the North Fork and its surroundings have remained remote and roadless,

Kromona Basin

free of both loggers and hikers. Loggers are still at work elsewhere in the basin, however, and a very recent clearcut faces the Kromona Mine Road to the east. Other slopes ringing the reservoir show traces of logging of the recent and not-so-recent past, including hills far too steep to have been cut in the first place.

At 3 miles there is a rough campsite at a wide point in the road. The forest becomes younger, perhaps twenty years old. Streams become fewer and farther between. At 3½ miles, while crossing a rockslide and negotiating some shallow ditches, I found two large boulders almost blocking the road. Just past the boulders the route enters a relic patch of old-growth timber.

Finally, at 4½ miles the road-end is reached. Here another wooden bridge has dramatically collapsed, and there is another rough campsite just before the rocks that mark the road's end.

Feeling curious, I left my bike to explore farther. I had read mention of the Kromona Mine and its outbuildings, and I wanted to see what might be left.

Not much, as it turned out. Climbing down the steep slope to the stream under the broken bridge, I was able to ford the water without difficulty. There is only the faintest trace of a route on the far side, marked by old blazes here and there.

I tried, first off, to find the spot where my map showed the mine itself. I climbed a rock field partway up the slope of the aptly named Prospect Peak, but abandoned the effort at a cliff and waterfall after finding only the odd piece of mine debris. I then followed the valley-floor stream up toward the headwall of the valley, but again was rewarded with nothing but bushes where my map showed a few buildings. This open area beneath Mount Stickney is beautiful and remote-feeling, but too brush-choked to offer much in the way of hiking or camping. The way down was fun—it took only 45 minutes on my bike. I saw no one the whole way, and little trace that visitors had been by any time in the recent past. Not bad for a trailhead only a bit over an hour from Seattle.

By Gary Faigin

33 DNR ROAD
RUGGED RIDGE VIEW

ONE TRENCH, TWO TRENCHES, THREE TRENCHES, FOUR . . .

Road status: Closed
Round trip: 5½ miles
High point: 3611 feet
Elevation gain: 1400 feet

Maps: Skykomish Ranger District and Green Trails: No. 142
Index

Take this hike to a panoramic viewpoint overlooking Spada Reservoir and you may find yourself afterward counting trenches in your sleep. I counted seventy-five on my way up—seventy-five energy-wasting, ugly, road-despoiling ditches (some as deep as 30 feet) that had to be climbed into and out of to reach the top. Sound tiring? Sound worth it? That depends on your attitude. The upside of this hike is complete and almost guaranteed solitude. It's likely no one else besides you would be crazy enough to negotiate all those ditches just to get up a hill, even with the great view.

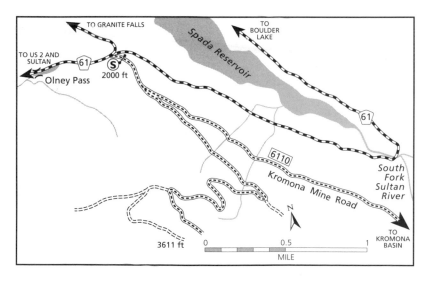

The downside, besides the aforementioned obstacles, is the sadly abused state of the land itself. That view comes at a price—there's a reason there are no trees to block it. The surrounding forest is struggling to make a comeback after having been mined off a slope far too steep to have been logged in the first place. You march up the road into a scene of increasing devastation. Logging debris and slash are strewn everywhere, landslides are numerous, and only the amazing resiliency of the forest hereabouts gives one any hope that the area may eventually green up, in a tattered sort of way.

Driving directions: To reach the Kromona Mine Road, turn left (north) on the Sultan Basin Road (Road 61) just east of the town of Sultan on US Highway 2. At 13.6 miles on the Sultan Basin Road there is a registration booth and a sign announcing the beginning of the Everett Watershed. Park in the large turnoff just past the booth, where the road forks. Here you will find the gated Kromona Mine Road, elevation 2000 feet.

The road to the Spada viewpoint starts as a spur road to the much more intact Kromona Mine Road, about ¼ mile past the entrance gate. The obstacles start immediately, with two large trenches dug to prevent vehicles from using the route. From then on the trenches are random and frequent, the result of the land managers' decision to pull all the culverts from under the road after it was abandoned.

Sometimes there are a few hundred feet between ditches, sometimes one immediately follows another. It can be very discouraging. There is little at this point to reward the hiker (the bikers having given up by now), not to mention the almost-continual sound of gunfire, coming from several locations below me the Sunday I walked the route. Who was shooting at what? I was never able to determine an answer. At least it wasn't me.

The road gains elevation and switchbacks upward, the first switchback coming at 1 mile, a dead-end spur continuing straight ahead. As the route contours up the hill, the forest thins, allowing views up to a scalped ridge whose trees were taken out via this very road. The trenches slowly begin to shallow out, and they become less and less troublesome the higher the path goes. At 1¼ miles, the road enters a log dump. The obvious road on the naked cliff 500 feet above you is your destination. A confusion of routes departs here; the correct route is the clearest road, rising up the hill to the northwest.

High point on a spur off Kromona Mine Road (photo by Gary Faigin)

A half mile past the log dump, an obvious spur departs sharply to the left. Keep right. Soon the route emerges from the trees onto the open edge of a cliff, and the views get more and more panoramic. Armed with a good map, no end of fun can be had picking out the peaks—Pilchuck, Bare Mountain, Marble Peak, Big Four, Vesper Peak, the Greider Ridge, Ragged Ridge, Mount Stickney. One can admire, too, the network of logging roads crisscrossing the Spada Basin, and recoil at other, more distant scalped ridges that are also slow in recovering from being turned into lumber.

Finally, turn back and head downward. Unfortunately, the trenches are no easier on the downhill route than the uphill, and you will not be sorry to have seen the last of them as you reach number seventy-five just before the junction with the Kromona Mine Road.

By Gary Faigin

34 DNR ROAD
WILLIAMSON CREEK

Road status: Closed
Round trip: 14 miles to Williamson Creek, 28 miles to road-end
High point: 2216 feet
Elevation gain: 500 feet

Maps: Skykomish Ranger District, Green Trails: Nos. 142 Index, 110 Silverton

Originally, the Williamson Creek mining road crossed the Sultan River on a concrete bridge and followed the creek for 4.5 miles, to the backside of Big Four Mountain and Marble Pass.

When Spada Reservoir flooded the bridge, a cliff-hanger road was built on the north side of the reservoir, with grand views looking down on the lake (reservoir) surrounded by high hills. After 7 tortuous miles, the road descended to Williamson Creek and views of glaciers and peaks. Unfortunately, when the road was decommissioned, numerous culverts were removed, leaving huge holes in the road that must be climbed into and then out of again.

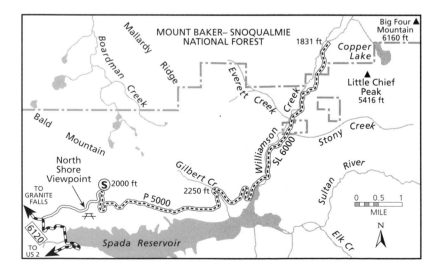

Driving directions: Take US Highway 2 out of Monroe, going east toward Sultan. As you head out of Sultan, on the left-hand side is a road with a sign that reads "Sultan Recreation Area"; this is Sultan Basin Road. Take the Sultan Basin Road about 14 miles to the Spada Lake Municipal Watershed Registration Area. You can register here and read some history about the area. Just past the registration area, turn left, taking the Pilchuck entry point entrance (there is a gate at this point that may be locked). Drive about a mile or so and cross the dam for the water supply for Everett. The view from the dam is beautiful, and the road to this point is great. Follow this road up the hill from the dam to a Y; keep right. (There's a gate in the road to the left.) Follow the road past the North Shore Viewpoint (great views from here, and bathrooms). Just past the North Shore Viewpoint, the road splits again. Keep to the right and park at the end of the road, elevation 2000 feet.

Take the road/trail that is at the very end of the drivable road and faces the lake. (This road can also be reached by the Pilchuck River Road

Willows are encroaching on an abandoned road

from Granite Falls.) There are three large ditches to hike through before you reach the main road. Dirt-bike riders use about the first 2 miles of the trail before giving up, due to the number of ditches that you have to cross. We averaged twenty-five ditches a mile, and hiked over 7 miles down the road. This was a round-trip total of 350 huge ditches that we hiked down into and then up the other side.

When the logging was done in this area, they left the road in an impassable condition. We rode our bikes and hiked the ditches 4 miles up the road to Gilbert Creek. This part of the trip is pretty and has great views of the lake. There is no bridge at Gilbert Creek, and in the spring and fall this creek crossing would be very dangerous.

The hike up Williamson Creek is wonderful and has great views of the valley and surrounding mountains. At about 7 miles in from the car, the ditches became too much work and we turned around. The hike back was long and hard.

If the ditches could be made passable with a bridge to make it across safely, this could be a great hike. The first 2 miles of the trip is worthwhile to reach some views of the lake, but there's not much more payoff until you get up into the Williamson Creek area. This hike in the fall and spring would be nice because of all the waterfalls and creeks. The ditches make this hike difficult to enjoy and get into a rhythm. If a hiker wants to hike big ditches all day and have a chance to see some bear and deer, this is a great hike to do. My recommendation is to make the road passable for hiking and biking.

By Carl Shanahan

Ira Spring's comment: While the road needed to be removed, in doing so the DNR obliterated a historic mining trail access to the backside of Big Four Mountain and beautiful blue-green Copper Lake. Certainly when the logging was done, they could have restored the trail while the road was being closed.

35 ROAD 6310
JUMPOFF RIDGE

Road status: Closed
Round trip: 8 miles
High point: 2600 feet
Elevation gain: 2300 feet

Maps: Skykomish Ranger District and Green Trails: No. 143
Monte Cristo

This is a very enjoyable hike. The 360-degree view at the top is tremendous—Mount Index, Mount Persis, Mount Baring, Gunn Peaks, Spire Mountain, and the North Skykomish River valley below. The road follows Bitter Creek for most of the way and you can hear it trickling or rumbling as you gradually ascend. I also liked the road because I was completely alone, on a Saturday in early summer, and that is getting more and more rare.

Driving directions: On US Highway 2 (Stevens Pass Highway), turn left (north) at milepost 35 onto the Index–Galena Road, which becomes

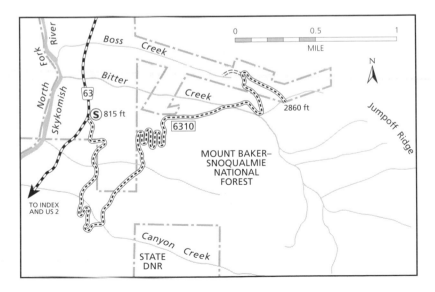

FS Road 63. In one mile, pass the town of Index, and in 3.9 miles from US Highway 2 find a small parking spot on the right by a gate and a "Road Closed" sign, elevation 815 feet.

Road 6310 is generally clear and there are no growth impediments, except for the last mile or so. It's a gradual climb (not steep or difficult, as switchbacks can be on trails). The Forest Service has done an excellent job of building roads. Of course, a road is much safer than a trail. I have been on some ridge trails only a foot wide, with sheer drops of 1000 feet. Here I feel I'm on solid ground, with no fear of falling. About 2 miles up, there are huge rocks in the road to prevent any trucks from continuing

Looking down the North Fork valley from Road 6310 (photo by Deborah Cooke)

on. This is a good spot for a camp-site, next to a waterfall.

I am surprised by the lack of mushrooms, but there are salmon-berry, wild fuchsia, devils club, and alder trees everywhere. I hear the Swainson's thrush and the show-offy winter wren warbling away. After 2½ miles of continuous ascent, there is a great view of the North Skykomish River valley below. There is no sign of civilization for miles and miles—no houses, no roads, no bridges, no trains—only the distant murmur of a plane. I dream I am an Indian, an old-time miner, a lumberjack or pioneer on the northwest edge of the world.

The road gradually deteriorates and becomes more like a trail. Alder, alder, everywhere. I recall a surprising statistic I read, that 60 to 70 percent of the forests in Washington are de-ciduous. I thought it would be co-

Vanilla leaf

niferous. Looking down at the forest below I see that it's true, primarily deciduous. This is my kind of place, alone in the wilderness. I continue upward, and I see another huge mountain in and out of the clouds.

I cross a talus slope and wonder if there are any marmots up in the rocks. I haven't seen any scat or tracks, or any sign of an animal.

For the first time I'm going down, which is a welcome change, and into an older forest. It feels more like a trail now and I like it. The road crosses the roaring Bitter Creek when I am almost out of the talus. Then the road continues up to the end, where there is a circular, cleared log-ging area. This is a good spot for an overnight, as it's flat and has great views. I feel I can almost touch the mountain, it's that close. The clouds clear and unveil the snowcovered mountain, where I see four huge waterfalls gushing down the cliffs. As I eat my lunch I hear the screech of a marmot.

A wonderful hike and not too hard. The solitude, the wilderness, and tremendous views make it well worthwhile.

By Deborah Cooke

36 ROAD 6321-010
IRON MOUNTAIN

Road status: Proposed to be closed
Round trip: 9 or 10 miles
High point: 4500 feet
Elevation gain: 3700 feet

Maps: Skykomish Ranger District and Green Trails: No.143
Monte Cristo

Although it's a steady climb, this rocky forest road leads to great vistas of mountains rarely seen from this angle. There are no other trails in this area, so this vista is little known.

Driving directions: From I-5, take US Highway 2 east to the Index–Galena Road (FS Road 63). Go 6.3 miles on the Index–Galena Road. Just past the Trout Creek bridge, take the road to the right (Road 6320). It is not gated. Drive ½ mile, passing a right spur that leads to a trashy campsite, to a junction. The left road climbs to Iron Mountain; the right road

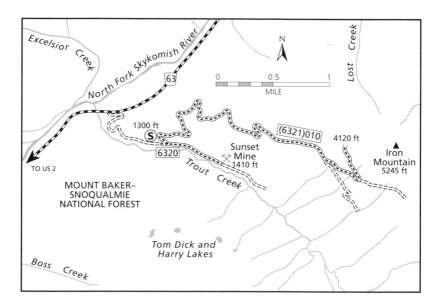

The author, even with the help of a ranger, was unable to identify this mountain (photo by Deborah Cooke)

takes you ½ mile to the Sunset Mine and a scramble trail to Tom Dick and Harry Lakes, where I hear the fishing is good. Park at the junction, elevation 1300 feet.

The Iron Mountain road is a hard climb, and the road feels like the bottom of a riverbed. I can't believe vehicles can drive up this road, but tread marks show they have. I have to watch where I'm walking, as there are rocks, ruts, and gullies. I look into the forest and think I see the dark

Bleeding heart

roof of a cabin, but it's only a fallen log. Older alders are along the road for most of the way, bending over to form gentle arches; they look as if they have woody eyes staring at me. I cross a creek with a dripping waterfall. If I were hot I'd stand under it, but it's still chilly on this first day of summer.

I think I'm at the top, but no such luck. Up and up and up. It's welcome to have soft dirt now beneath my feet. I haven't seen one footprint, but still see tire marks. How can any truck get up here? At a turn in the road, I see rips in the bark of a tree left by a bear sharpening its claws. Hope it's not near. I continue climbing and see old silver tree stumps, silent as graves.

Finally, I am at the top, where there are cliffs and huge rocks. There's a hawk soaring above, as I look, stunned, at the spectacular snow-topped mountains to the west, south, and north. I can see a dozen mountains and try to identify them from my map. Past the waterfall at the top are two excellent campsites. The road continues on, but I'm tired. I almost hate reaching the top, because it means I will be going back, retracing my steps.

I now understand why "the getting there" takes so much longer than the return. It's because I don't know what to expect, and in returning, I do. Climbing down, I've worked up a sweat, so I take the plunge under the dripping waterfall. It's freezing and wonderful. I can hear the river below and know I am almost to my car. I see what I think is a large dark dog up ahead, but it's a bear. When he sees me, he immediately fades into the forest. I've seen several bears on my hikes and they have all acted like this. They just saunter away. I start singing in a loud voice and scurry on down the road. There is nothing better after a hike than to come back to my car, exhausted, but safe and elated.

By Deborah Cooke

37 ROAD 6334
MINERAL BUTTE

Road status: Proposed to be closed
Round trip: 6 miles
High point: 3400 feet
Elevation gain: 2200 feet

Maps: Skykomish Ranger District and Green Trails: No. 143
Monte Cristo

I like going on off-off roads. It makes an adventurer out of me, an ordinary person. Especially this road, with views that really open up at the top, of mountains that have been seen by few people from this angle. I look at the map and notice there are no other trails in this area. There is little water on this road.

Driving directions: From I-5, take US Highway 2 east to the Index–Galena Road (FS Road 63). Go 9.2 miles on the Index–Galena Road and, just past the Howard Creek bridge, take a left on the Salmon Creek road,

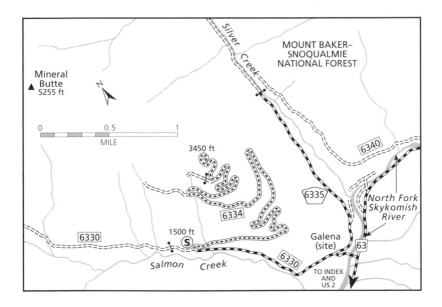

Unidentified mountain from Road 6334 (photo by Deborah Cooke)

No. 6330. Cross over the South Fork Skykomish bridge. At 1.4 miles up the Salmon Creek Road, park your car at the junction with Road 6334, to the left, elevation 1500 feet.

▲▲

   This road looks very drivable for the first mile or so, but since there are few turnarounds, it's best to park your car as suggested. The road is not gated. It's a very gradual ascent, and quite an easy hike. After a mile, there's another road to the right, which I explored. It led into the dark forest to a huge clearing with pondlike puddles, with hundreds of tadpoles and water bugs. Since this road eventually peters out into brush, I went back to the main road. It becomes very rocky, and I miss a dirt trail. I can't tell how high I am, because trees along the road block my view. It's shady and comforting.

After 2 miles, there is an opening in the trees, and I notice for the first time Mineral Butte, which is an extremely unusual mountain, with turrets and spires of stone, at 5255 feet high. I can't get over how stony it is here—remnants left by the glacial till. I'm going higher, but it's an easy climb, and look at the bright green grass, stretching to the sun. There are huckleberry, salmonberry, and trillium. There is no other sign of life, no trash, no tread marks, no footprints, no scat. I feel very safe, even though I am quite high, with huge, immense space all around, and pristine-pure, snowcovered mountains in the distance. I see Monte Cristo to the north and Mount Index to the south. It's remarkable to think that very few people have seen these mountains, near a huge city like Seattle. (I almost don't want to tell you where this road is, but that's selfish of me.)

Dogwood tree blossoms

I quickly return to my car and drive down to the bridge crossing the North Fork Skykomish River. The river is named after the Indian tribe; the name means "upriver people." The river is famous for white-water rafting, but it's also very dangerous. I notice there is a mining claim on the right by the bridge, and also a path going into the forest. I walk the trail, which ends at a grave with "R.I.P." written with stones. Rest in peace, whoever you are. Yesterday I saw another grave marker, of a four-year-old girl who drowned in Troublesome Creek, farther up the river. Yet another memorial, opposite the nearby San Juan Campground, reads, "Mom, we miss you." Please be careful.

By Deborah Cooke

38 ROAD 6335
MINERAL CITY AND POODLE DOG PASS

Road status: Closed

TO MINERAL CITY
Round trip: 7 miles
High point: 2173 feet
Elevation gain: 800 feet

TO POODLE DOG PASS AND SILVER LAKE
Round trip: 15 miles
High point: 4350 feet
Elevation gain: 2950 feet

Maps: Skykomish Ranger District and Green Trails: No. 143
Monte Cristo

Walk a road, gated by a perpetual rockslide, to the site of once-prosperous Mineral City, which boasted of two hotels. Go on to views, following a rugged, mostly abandoned trail to Poodle Dog Pass. If the pass is

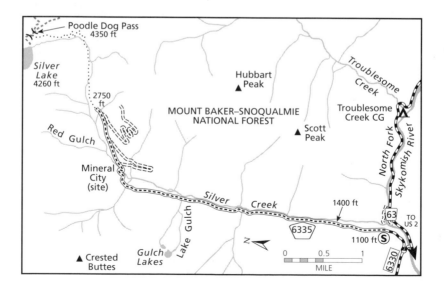

your destination, there is a much easier trail by way of the Monte Cristo road. *Note:* The rockslide may have moved again and could be dangerous. Also, all the bridges are rotting and could collapse. Take this hike at your own risk.

Driving directions: From I-5, take US Highway 2 east to the Index–Galena Road (FS Road 63). Go left on the Index–Galena Road and drive 9.2 miles. Just past the Howard Creek bridge, take a left on Road 6330. Cross over the North Fork Skykomish bridge and, in 0.1 mile, go right on the Snohomish County Mine-to-Market Road 6335. It is possible to drive another 1.5 miles, but between 0.2 mile and 0.6 mile the road is badly

Old mine along Mineral Creek

eroded and only passable to a car with high clearance. There is a deep wash 600 feet from a barricade that marks the end of the road, elevation 1400 feet.

At the road-end, the way turns into a trail and shortly enters a massive rockslide that is in two parts. People live on the numerous claims along the way and have scratched a thin tread across the slides, which change from year to year.

My wife and I rode our bicycles to Mineral City. Our problem was crossing the perpetual rockslide. We are a bit shaky, so we walked the bicycles across, but, even so, it was scary. A crumpled motorbike on the rocks beside Silver Creek didn't make us feel any better.

Except for a rotting bridge and a few blowdowns to climb over, beyond the second slide the old roadbed is a joy. The way is in sound of Silver Creek, and mostly in sight as well. There was nothing left of the hotels and mill that once stood at Mineral City. However, the location makes a good campsite.

From there the way turned mean, and we hid our bicycles. We took a steep, badly eroded truck road upward and were compensated with views. The red slash across the way was aptly named Red Gulch.

In a very short mile the road switchbacked to the left, climbing high to what must be great views. We picked up the Poodle Dog Pass trail, but we were too early in the season and were stopped by the rushing torrent of Silver Creek at snowmelt time. We would have liked to explore the road above the switchback to see if the views were really good, but it was still snowcovered in late June.

The Skykomish District map shows a continuous patchwork of mining property given away by the antiquated 1800s mining law. The land was private, which explains the atrocious logging that took place.

By Ira Spring

39 ROAD 6574
SAN JUAN HILL

Road status: Closed and left impassable
Round trip: 5 miles
High point: 4100 feet
Elevation gain: 700 feet

Maps: Skykomish Ranger District and Green Trails: No. 143
Monte Cristo

There are views, views that are best described as *wow*!

This road was decommissioned in August 2000 in such a way that 20- to 30-foot pits were left in the road, making hiking virtually impassible. Fortunately, I was able to walk the road before the Forest Service tore it up so badly that it may be impossible to use.

Driving directions: From either the North Fork Skykomish River road (most is paved) or the Beckler River road, drive to Jack Pass and go uphill on Road 6570 for 0.7 mile. At this point, Road 6570 makes a steep

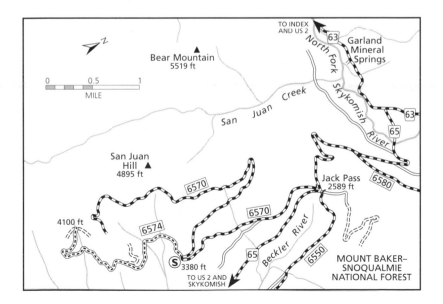

switchback and No. 6574 goes straight ahead—the start of the decommissioned Road 6574, elevation 3380 feet.

Views: In ¼ mile, look south to a sharp pyramid-shaped peak, which might (or might not) be 6190-foot Mount Fernow. At ½ mile the sharp pyramid is a better view, and to the north, Kyes Peak looms up. In a short mile is a switchback with added views to the south of Mount Hinman and Mount Daniels.

The higher one goes, the better the views get. At 1½ miles, Glacier Peak pokes over a hilltop. At 2 miles is a second switchback, with views of the whole Monte Cristo range and those mountains around Glacier Peak. But keep going, as just around the next switchback the Dutch Miller Gap peaks show up.

I didn't get any farther, for a steep snowbank without runoff covered the road that last week of June. However, the map shows the road climbing higher on the rounded (and logged) end of San Juan Hill.

By Ira Spring

Keyes Peak, taken a month before the road was decommissioned

40 ROAD 6554
15 TRIALS OF HERCULES (EVERGREEN MOUNTAIN)

Road status: Closed
Round trip: 9 miles
High point: 4400 feet
Elevation gain: 600 feet

Maps: Skykomish Ranger District and Green Trails: No. 143
Monte Cristo

I can think of only one sensible reason to walk this road, much less bike it: to see what is at the end. Unless you are training for extreme mountain biking, the hurdles found on this road are not much worth the effort. But if you want to go somewhere no one else has the sense to go, this is the trail for you. Another road/trail destroyed in the summer of 2000.

Driving directions: From I-5, take US Highway 2 to the Index–Galena Road (FS Road 63). Stay on the Index–Galena Road to a four-way intersection; go straight ahead, on FS Road 65. Reach Jack Pass and another

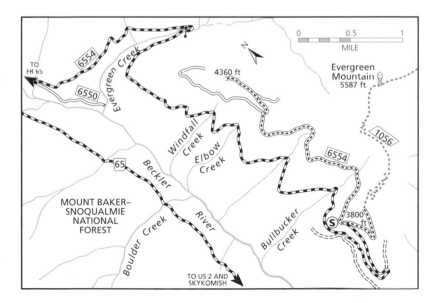

Evergreen Mountain Lookout

four-way junction 17 miles from US 2. Take FS Road 6550. Follow it for a mile, then take a left on FS Road 6554. In 2 more miles is a gate. The road was supposed to be closed until fall of 2001, but now you should be able to drive the 7 more miles to the trailhead. Park at the second to the last switchback before the Evergreen Mountain trailhead. This is where you start bicycling, elevation 3800 feet.

This road used to be a pleasant bicycle ride, with a stunning view of Mount Rainier down the Beckler River Valley. The view is still there, but it is now an arduous trek, crossing fifteen gullies up to 30 feet deep, with 6- to 8-foot berms, where culverts once diverted water under the road. Then, to finish it off, the road was plowed up for another couple hundred yards. Where the plowing starts is a fork in the road that, either way you go, circles around a knoll. If you've stumbled this far, you may as well see what is at the end of the road, which, from this point on, is smooth and unencumbered.

On the way back you will have plenty of time to think about taking the foot trail up to the Evergreen Mountain Lookout, less then a couple miles from where you started.

By Tom Karchesy

41 ROAD 6516-110
KLINGER RIDGE

Road status: Open to high-clearance vehicles
Round trip: 4 miles
High point: 4494 feet
Elevation gain: 1000 feet

Maps: Skykomish Ranger District; Green Trails: Nos. 143 Monte
Cristo and 175 Skykomish

This trip can certainly be described as having a very high "pleasure-to-pain" ratio. Although the 4494-foot summit is heavily treed and offers no views, the route up has many spots to stop and enjoy the scenery. To the south, the views continue to expand until, at the 1½-mile point, there is almost a 180-degree panorama across the Skykomish River, which includes Mount Daniel, Mount Hinman, Chimney, and a myriad of other peaks in the Alpine Lakes area. For those inclined to visit the summit, it provides a nice shady spot to eat lunch. Exploring in the summit area one can find some peekaboo views to the north, one of which provides a narrowly framed look at Townsend Mountain.

Driving directions: To get there from I-5, drive east on US Highway 2.

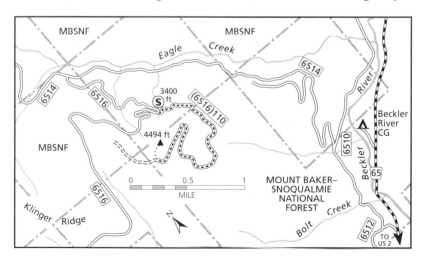

Merchant Peak from Klinger Ridge (photo by Jim Baker)

About ½ mile east of the town of Skykomish, turn left on the Beckler River Road.

After only 0.6 mile, turn left on Road 6510. In another mile take Road 6514 to the left. This climbs out of the Beckler valley and heads northwesterly up the Eagle Creek drainage, with a beautiful gorge on the right and Eagle Rock hovering above to the north. In 3.7 miles is a junction with Road 6516. Take this hard left and, in 1.2 miles, you'll arrive at Road 6516-110. (At this point you are 6.5 miles from Highway 2.) There is room here to park several cars. The road/trail is blocked to car traffic by debris, elevation 3400 feet.

A good tread here with a moderate gradient, about 500 feet per mile, should appeal to almost everyone. Much of the terrain has been cut over but is softened somewhat by the newer growth that is flourishing. Occasionally the route passes through larger timber, probably second growth. Activity of loggers in the past has provided numerous unobstructed view spots, where landings were constructed to facilitate "yarding" in the logs.

Take your camera! Good maps and a compass can help you identify the riches to the south. If you did not look back in the first ½ mile of your ascent, on your return you will discover great views of Merchant and Townsend Peaks up the Eagle drainage to the north.

Enjoy—how could you not!

By Jim Baker

42 ROADS 6522, 6526, AND 6527
JOHNSON RIDGE

Road status: Road 6522 open because gate is vandalized; all
other spurs are closed
Round trip: 2 to 6 miles
High points: 3800 feet to 4830 feet
Elevation gain: 200 feet to 1400 feet

Maps: Skykomish Ranger District and Green Trails: No. 143
Monte Cristo

Why would anyone choose an abandoned road with modest views instead of the "real" Johnson Ridge trail, with in-season flower fields and at all seasons exciting views of the Monte Cristo Peaks, Glacier Peak, and a view into the Eagle Rock roadless and trails area?

The best reason for walking these abandoned roads is solitude, virtually guaranteed. Or maybe just because it's there. Furthermore, the nearby Johnson Ridge trail is open to motorcycles. While 4½ miles one way is a days' recreation for a hiker, it represents only a half-hour ride to a motorcyclist, and isn't worth the effort of driving to the trailhead. However, if you were unlucky enough to arrive at the Johnson Ridge trailhead on a day when motorcycles were present, one of these abandoned roads might look very attractive.

Driving directions: Drive US Highway 2 to Skykomish. Just 0.2 mile east of the town, turn left on Beckler River Road No. 65. At 6.8 miles, turn right on Road 6520, possibly signed "Johnson Creek" and "Johnson Ridge Trail" (sign missing at time of research). At a junction 1.7 miles from Beckler River Road, keep straight ahead, and at 5.6 miles, turn right on Road 6526 and drive to its end some 7 miles from Beckler River, elevation 3620 feet. (Don't be confused by a spur road 0.3 mile from the road-end.)

Road 6526: Of the three closed roads on Johnson Ridge, Pat and I only explored the mile-long Road 6526, because it offered the best view. It should have been a pleasant walk with nice views and flowers, but in the process of decommissioning the roadbed, the Forest Service pulled out the side-cast material and piled it on the road bed in a haphazard way that made walking difficult. With the power equipment on hand, how easy it would have been to leave an 18-inch walkway across the top.

Pulling back the side-cast and digging out the culverts is the environmental way of decommissioning a road. However, Washington Trails Association (WTA) and the local chapter of the Sierrra Club and I had urged that a narrow foot/bicycle tread be left in the dirt piles. It wasn't done here, and for a third of the distance walking was tedious, although the road certainly affords solitude and fair views.

Road 6527: We did not walk Road 6527, although it looks fairly level. It's about 2 miles to Johnson Creek and possible camps.

Road 6522: By car we explored Road 6522, leading to the scalped 4600-foot ridge of a private tree farm on the east side of Johnson Creek. The Forest Service map showed the road gated where it enters private land at 3360 feet. However, the gate had been vandalized and the road is

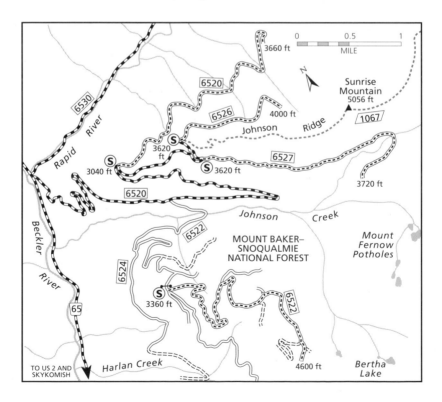

Abandoned Road 6526

open all the way to the top. At about 4000 feet the road became too rough for our car. Oh! But the views! The Monte Cristo Peaks, and south to Eagle Rock, Baring, Gunn Peak, Merchant Peak, and a bunch we couldn't name. Remember this is a private road and private land. If a keep-out sign is ever erected—keep out.

By Ira Spring

43 ROAD 6550
BECKLER RIVER

Road status: Closed
Round trip: 2 to 4 miles
High point: 2000 feet
Elevation loss: 100 feet to 1900 feet at Elbow Creek (site of the
   wonderful camp), down to as much as 1500 feet beyond that

Maps: USGS: Evergreen Mtn. Quadrangle and Green Trails: No.
   143 Monte Cristo

Sometimes you just want an easy hike or bike ride to a perfect camp,
where you can unload your gear and just go exploring. This is a perfect
family trail with plenty of wilderness to enjoy.

Driving directions: From I-5, take US Highway 2 to the Index–Galena
Road (FS Road 63). After the Index–Galena Road becomes dirt, there is a
fork. Take FS Road 65, straight ahead. Reach Jack Pass and a four-way

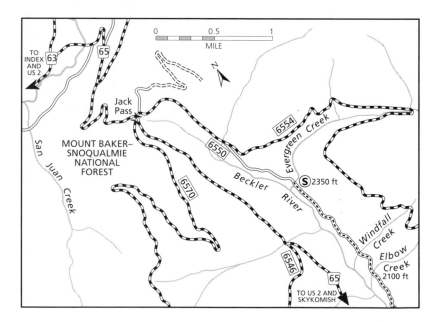

junction 17 miles from US 2. Keep straight ahead on FS Road 6550, and enjoy the view of the valley on your right. You'll start downhill and pass the turnoff (to the left) to Evergreen Mountain (FS Road 6554), but keep on Road 6550 and soon you will come where it ends, at Evergreen Creek (18.5 miles). Turn your car around and park it on the side of the road, elevation 2350 feet.

The most difficult part of the trip is getting across Evergreen Creek. Early in the season it can be up to 4 feet high, but you can get around that by going upstream and crossing on a log. Bring a safety rope and take care; the logs can be slippery. Look carefully along the riverbank for what looks to be a den, facing upstream under a tree near one of the crossing logs. Remember that it may be someone's home.

Once on the road/trail, you'll find it perfect for biking. You'll cross a few reclaimed streams, where the culverts have been removed and revegetation efforts have been made. At about a mile you will come to a clearing of velvet moss with a couple fire rings. Here you can see up Evergreen Mountain and some nearby hills. Some may complain that there is a lack of views, but it is well compensated by the proximity of a good water supply (Elbow Creek) and the surprising absence of annoying insects. This is a good place to pitch camp and go on further to explore the flora

The author beside Beckler River (photo by Tom Karchesy)

Fir trees

and fauna of the river valley. Keep a clean camp and be sure to follow good practices of separating your camp, cooking, and food storage area—you're in bear country.

Just as you enter the camp area, if you go back across the road into the trees, you will find a couple of trees that look pretty much mauled, by I don't know what—insects, bears, or something in between. Cross Elbow Creek, staying a little to the right, and you will come back onto the road/trail, thick with alder saplings. In a short time, though, you will reach a smooth, open road that seems to follow the river, and eventually fades into the hillside after a few miles. Watch out for small holes in the road that could catch an unwary foot.

By Tom Karchesy

44 ROAD 6028
BARING MOUNTAIN

Road status: Open to ORVs
Round trip: 1 to 3½ miles
High point: 2320 feet
Elevation gain: 200 feet to 1530 feet

Maps: Skykomish Ranger District and Green Trails: No. 143
    Monte Cristo

Dazzling views of majestic Mount Persis and Mount Index, and the sublime beauty of the South Fork Skykomish River valley are offerings for the adventuresome hiker who reaches the end of this obscure Forest Service road.

Speeding through Baring, elevation 790 feet, on US Highway 2 at 60mph does not offer the driver or passengers an appreciation of the surrounding landscape. For a bird's-eye view, take a short drive, followed by an even shorter hike, on FS Road 6028. This old Forest Service road offers

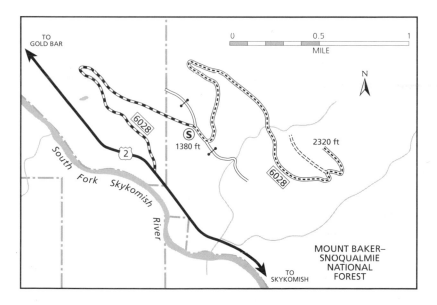

Mount Index from Road 6028 (photo by Jan Klippert)

an opportunity to see some magnificent country, and is open year round either for hiking or snowshoeing .

Driving directions: About 2 miles east of Baring on US 2, on the eastern approach of the bridge that crosses the Burlington Northern railroad, turn north onto FS Road 6028.

The surface of this old logging road is in pretty good shape. At about 1 mile, cross under the main Bonneville transmission lines. The transmission line clearcut gives a wonderful view to the east, where Malachite Peak, Cleveland Mountain, and the South Fork Skykomish River basin come into view.

At 1.5 miles from US 2, FS Road 6028 has been decommissioned. Park here, elevation 1380 feet. Beyond that point, brush is encroaching upon the road. The tread is pretty good, but the adventuresome driver should proceed only if he doesn't care about the vehicle's paint job.

The road is drivable for another mile or so to a well-used camping site. It has a good water supply. The road grade increases for the next half mile to the end of the logging road. Once you've achieved this high point, there are extensive views of the mountains extending from Persis and Index easterly to Malachite. Elevation at the turnaround is 2320 feet.

It is about 3.5 miles from US Highway 2 to the end of the logging road, 3 miles to the campsite. Although not rugged terrain, this abandoned logging road could offer several opportunities for the hiking enthusiast. It would be good for children, and a welcome early spring outing. As US 2 is open throughout the winter months, FS Road 6028 could provide a great snowshoe outing. There is an adequate pull-off area on the side of US 2 for those wanting to snowshoe FS Road 6028. Mountain bikes are also a viable option.

Views of the valley on a clear day make the walk memorable.

Exploring Baring, with its beautiful mountains as a scenic backdrop, is well worthwhile. Cross the one-lane suspension bridge on the Index Creek Road. Stop on US Highway 2 a mile west of Baring, at milepost 39, to enjoy spectacular Sunset Falls. It is the site of an old quarry. Tumbling water and pools are awesome and well worth the short hike from the road to the falls. And, if there is enough time left in the day, take the 2-mile walk to Barclay Lake, elevation 2622 feet. The Barclay Lake Trail, elevation 2200 feet, starts at the end of FS Road 6124, which starts in the town of Baring.

By Jan Klippert

45 ROAD 6410
WEST FORK MILLER RIVER

Road status: Deteriorated county mine-to-market road; county plans to close

TO CONEY CREEK
Round trip: 4½ miles
High point: 2000 feet
Elevation gain: 650 feet

TO CONEY BASIN
Round trip: 6½ miles
High point: 2700 feet
Elevation gain: 1450 feet

Maps: Skykomish Ranger District and Green Trails: No. 175 Skykomish

Cascading West Fork Miller River waters roar as constant companions on this deteriorated mine-to-market road. Walking on much of the old road, identified as FS Road 6410, is now like walking on an uneven, well-worn streambed. Weather and water have eroded much of the road that is now the hiker's tread. The old road parallels the West Fork Miller River. There are no really outstanding views of the mountains, but the hiker is rewarded with several views of the tumultuous course of the Miller River and an occasional view of the surrounding mountain peaks. This is remote country. Solitude. The valley is removed from the hurry-up of the very popular Lake Dorothy/East Fork Miller River, east of the 5500-foot ridge separating the two valleys. This could serve as an easily accessible objective for early season hiking. As this lies deep in more re-mote areas of the Cascades, it may offer snowshoe opportunities when the Lake Dorothy Road opens in early spring. The tread appears to be too treacherous for equestrians.

Driving directions: West of Skykomish, US Highway 2 intersects the Old Cascade Highway at the Money Creek Campground. Travel southerly on the Old Cascade Highway about 1½ miles. At the intersection, go left on the Miller River Road (FS Road 6410) and drive another 4 miles. On the right side of the road, just before the one-lane bridge over the West Fork Miller River, is an old abandoned mine-to-market road. The more obvious road goes straight ahead, to the Lake Dorothy trailhead. There is a small space to park here at the fork in the road, elevation 1350 feet.

There is a camping spot near the parking area. In about ¼ mile there is another spacious and well-used campsite next to the river. The old road is now almost totally deteriorated. Generally the slopes, whether uphill or downhill, are eroded and rock-strewn. The more level stretches are easy walking.

Most streams along the way are easily crossed. However, the hiker will encounter two major streams that need to be forded. There are no stepping stones for crossing these streams, which are swollen from rain or snowmelt much of the hiking season.

At 1½ miles you'll encounter a giant cedar. Once again the road turns into river rubble for another ⅓ mile, as it continues deeper into the Cascade Range.

At 2.2 miles, flagging announces the intersection with the old Coney Mine access road. The road is not visible and has become overgrown with heavy brush. Flagging shows the way, and routefinding skills will be needed to follow the portion of long-abandoned road. Following the flags and working through the brush, you will eventually reach the Coney Creek basin, surrounded by 5700-foot peaks. At the end of the abandoned road

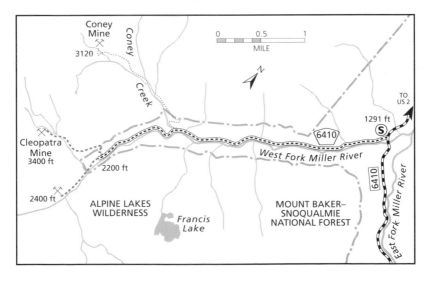

Rotting mine entrance along the old mine-to-market road

is the old mining camp, and mining artifacts. Here the adventurer will be rewarded with magnificent views of the basin and its precipitous granite walls and towering ridges.

At 3.6 miles is the Cleopatra Mine camp. The main road continues for another mile or so to the end. At one point, about ¼ mile before the end of the road, there is immediate access to the river and a large granite rock in the midst of a rapid. At the road-end, shooters have left much debris, including spent shotgun and brass cartridges. There is evidence of a trail crossing the river a little beyond the road-end.

Interesting mining history and spectacular granite cliffs surrounding the Miller River watersheds offset the inconsistency of the road's surface. The Miller River basin opened to prospecting in the late 1880s. At first, prospectors carried ore out by mule. Then the first wagon road was built in 1901. Mining became more important in the Miller River watershed when the Great Northern Railroad line was completed across Stevens Pass. During the mid-1950s, mining activities stopped. The roads have been unmaintained since that time. Remnants of mining activity and exploration of the area are interesting aspects of this forgotten road. For more complete information, *Discovering Washington's Historic Mines, Volume 1: The West Central Cascade Mountains* (Northwest Underground Explorations, Oso Publishing Company; Arlington, WA: 1997) is recommended reading and gives full details of mining activity in the area.

By Jan Klippert

46 GREAT NORTHERN RAILROAD
IRON GOAT TRAIL

Road status: Closed since 1929
Distance: ¼ mile to 6.6 miles one way
High point: 3143 feet
Elevation gain or loss: 500 feet

Maps: Skykomish Ranger District and Green Trails: Nos. 144
Benchmark Mtn. and 176 Stevens Pass

Only one of the three state historic wagon and railroad trails are preserved for hikers. The old Milwaukee Railroad over Snoqualmie Pass is, in reality, a gated road. The old Naches Wagon Trail is overwhelmed and clobbered by ORVs. Only the old 1893 Great Northern Railroad over Stevens Pass has sections that are still intact.

For the first four years, the railroad switchbacked over the pass, taking 12 miles of track to go 2.6 air miles from Berne on the east side to Wellington on the west side. Bits and pieces of this route can still be found. In 1900, a 2.6-mile tunnel under the pass was built. Although the tunnel made winter travel easier, avalanche hazard on the west side still remained, and in 1910 a giant avalanche originating on Windy Ridge carried

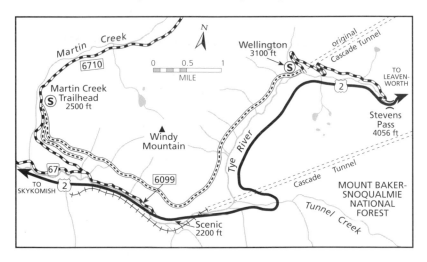

Wellington tunnel

two passenger trains parked in Wellington into the Tye Valley, killing 96 passengers. In 1929 the present 7.8-mile tunnel was opened, and the first tunnel and track from Wellington to Scenic was abandoned.

With the help of the government and private corporations, over ten years some 2000 volunteers worked on the 6.6-mile section from Wellington to Martin Creek. It was converted into one of the best interpretive trails in the West.

At this time there is a trailhead at both ends, and eventually there will be a third trailhead at Scenic. Both of the present trailheads offer easy hikes to points of interest. If transportation can be arranged, this is an excellent one-way trip. Although it is only a 2.2-percent grade, logic says start at Wellington and walk downhill to Marten Creek.

Driving directions: For the Wellington trailhead, drive US Highway 2 (Stevens Pass Highway) to Stevens Pass. If coming from the west, turn around and head back west. On the curve just west of Stevens Pass, go right on the old Stevens Pass Highway for 2.8 miles, and then turn right again, to the parking lot and rest room, elevation 3100 feet.

For the Martin Creek trailhead, drive US Highway 2 6 miles west of the town of Skykomish. At milepost 55, go left on Road 67, a segment of the old Stevens Pass Highway, for 2.3 miles, then turn left again on Forest Road 6710 and drive another 1.4 miles to the trailhead, elevation 2500 feet. At either trailhead, start walking, and feel the ghosts that live along the railroad grade.

By Ira Spring

47 MOUNT WASHINGTON

Road status: Closed
Round trip: 12 miles, allow 8 hours
High point: 4800 feet
Elevation gain: 3400 feet

Maps: North Bend Ranger District and Green Trails: No. 206
Bandera

Like two great sentinels, Mount Si and Mount Washington stand guard over the North Bend entrance to the Cascades. Thanks to an excellent trail, Mount Si is a well-known hikers' destination, with a massive parking area, a waiting line for the bathroom, and a steady parade of people heading to the summit. Mount Washington, with views that surpass those found on Mount Si, never has had a formal trail to the summit, so hikers will be rewarded with peace and solitude.

Mount Washington stands at the end of a long line of clearcut summits overlooking the Cedar River Watershed. For years, private land ownership and the proliferation of roads kept interest in this area to a minimum. Now, in conjunction with the Iron Horse Trail, and with the help of a lot of volunteers, a basic trail has been sketched in across the lower slopes of the mountain, tying old and often overgrown roads together. The upper sections show signs of more recent logging, and the trail route follows a series of well-defined roadbeds along the ridge crests.

The circuitous combination of trail and abandoned logging roads, maintained and marked by dedicated volunteers, can lead to some confusion. Occasionally markers are moved, and hikers have been known to wander. When hiking to the summit for the first time, either follow the directions step by step, or head out with a complete *laissez faire* attitude and just see where you end up. Whatever system you follow, take note of the twists and turns on the way up so that you can find your way back. Also, unless you have hours to devote to retracing your steps if you end up in the wrong place, do your exploring on the way up.

Driving directions: Drive east from the Puget Sound basin, or west from the rest of the world, on Interstate 90. Leave the freeway at Exit 38.

If coming from the Puget Sound side, turn right, then in a few hundred feet go right again for a short ascent to a large parking area, elevation 1200 feet. From the east, at the end of the exit ramp go left on old US Highway 10 and head downvalley 1.9 miles before turning left for the final 0.2 mile to the parking area. (*Note:* If you are planning to watch the sunset from the summit, park along the highway and walk up. The parking lot is gated at night and cars are impounded.)

From the parking lot, head up the steepish trail. After a short climb, the trail intersects a road and ends. Go right and continue up the final few feet to the Iron Horse Trail. Turn right, downvalley, on the old railroad grade. After a few hundred feet, pass a small, seasonal creek. A few feet beyond, a well-graveled trail heads into the dense brush. Do not waste time looking for a sign. At this and at all subsequent intersections, you must look for clues left by earlier visitors or simply rely on your instinct.

The trail heads straight toward the valley wall, where it turns and follows an old road. Head uphill on the first of several steep switchbacks. The old road skims along the edge of steep cliffs, passing fern grottos and even a spot where the water streams out of solid rock.

Two intersections are passed during the first mile. Stay right at both, leaving the left forks for the climbers with ropes and harnesses. At the end of 2 long miles in the forest, the trail reaches a partially overgrown

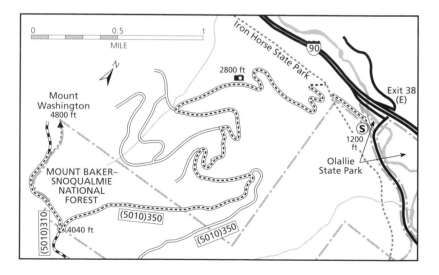

Vicky Spring on top of Mount Washington, Mount Rainier in the background
(photo by Tom Kirkendall)

viewpoint, elevation 2800 feet. With determination and a lot of standing on tiptoes, you can glimpse North Bend, Interstate 90, and Rattlesnake Mountain.

The trail continues to the left on a nearly level traverse. After ¼ mile is an intersection. Straight ahead is Mount Washington. However, despite the good-looking footpath heading in that direction, the best way to go is to the left. (The other trail is worth exploring, and the adventurous can reach the summit that way, if they have a good map and do not mind bushwhacking up a couple of steep hillsides.)

The correct trail now traverses up a brushy hillside, heading farther away from the summit with each step. At 2¾ miles, the brush-covered road you have been following intersects a more recently abandoned road. Go left, heading northeast around the hillside. Look back as you walk away from the intersection and pick out a landmark, or create one from rocks if you think you might miss it on the way back down.

The road climbs around the hillside into a clearcut basin. Walk past the tempting spur on the right and continue straight to intersect another road at 3¾ miles. Go left and descend 10 feet to a second intersection, then go right and continue the long traverse around the ridge. The road grade now improves to the point where ORVs can use it. Occasional fire rings are passed, indicating use by hunters. The road grade mellows, the major climb having been completed, and views open to the north and east as you go.

After a long traverse of the clearcut hillside, the road descends briefly, then skims the crest of a razor-sharp ridge before climbing to an intersection at the crest of a forested ridge at 5¼ miles, elevation 4040 feet. Go left and follow a grass-covered road along the crest of the ridge. Signs to the left indicate the boundary of the Cedar Watershed and warn of penalties for venturing beyond the road.

After a level ½-mile stroll, the road divides. Go straight ahead to find the trail going up a steep slope between the two roads. The trail follows the ridge crest, which in season is a lovely subalpine garden.

The trail ends at an old abandoned tower with a perfect rock for your picnic, elevation 4800 feet, and views of Mount Rainier, Chester Morse Reservoir, Cedar Lake, Interstate 90, the Olympics, all the Middle Fork and South Fork summits, and even the tip of Mount Stuart.

By Vicky Spring

48 ROAD 9020
MOUNT GARDNER

Road status: Undecided

TO VIEWPOINT
Round trip: 3 miles
High point: 3300 feet
Elevation gain: 1000 feet

TO ROAD-END
Round trip: 6 miles
High point: 3800 feet
Elevation gain: 1500 feet

Maps: North Bend Ranger District and Green Trails: No. 206
Bandera

One of the most dramatic views of the I-90 corridor. But the access road is a nightmare for a family car, and the walking portion is still open to high-centered four-wheel-drive vehicles.

Driving directions: Drive east on I-90 to Exit 39 and go right on the

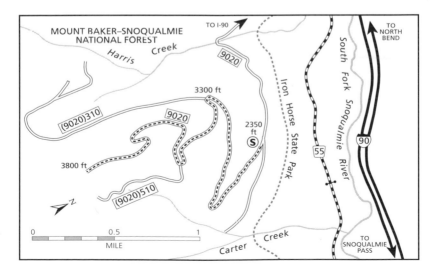

I-90 and the South Fork Snoqualmie River valley

former US Highway 10. In a short 2 miles, just before the east exit of 39 to I-90, go right on Forest Road 9020. The Forest Service inherited this road in a Weyerhaeuser land exchange, and little maintenance has occurred.

⸻

Within 0.3 mile is a humongous mud puddle that may not be passable until August. In 1 mile the road crosses the Iron Horse Trail. At 2.6 miles, pass the McClellan Butte trail, and, at about 3 miles, cross Alice Creek. Up to here the road is in fair shape. However, from Alice Creek on, the road alternates between fair, awful, and atrocious. At 6.1 miles the road turns steeply upward, the stopping point for the family car, elevation 2350 feet.

Heavy-duty four-wheel-drive vehicles bounce their way upward over boulders but, except during hunting season, few are seen. Walking is easy, though steep. While there are short sections of boulders that stop cars, most of the road/trail is in good shape. At ½ mile is a switchback. Views begin in a long mile as the road crosses a rockslide that is visible from I-90.

At 1½ miles, elevation 3300 feet, the way reaches a junction, a great place to contemplate Mother Nature's mountains rising above man-made clearcuts, powerline swaths, the old railroad grade, logging roads, and I-90, from Mount Si to Snoqualmie Pass.

The views do not get any better, but there is more to see. At the junction, the right fork goes into the wide Harris Creek Valley. Go left in a short half mile to a second junction. The left fork traverses the east side of Mount Gardner with no special view. The right fork climbs higher on Mount Gardner and ends at the Cedar River Watershed boundary, elevation 3800 feet, 3 miles from the car. From here is a striking view of the rugged cliffs of 5087-foot Mount Kent, rising above the 4703-foot cliffs of an unnamed ridge.

By Ira Spring

49 ROADS 5510-120, 5510-110, AND 5510-510
HUMPBACK MOUNTAIN

Maps: North Bend Ranger District and Green Trails: No. 206
Bandera

On a scale of one to ten, these views would only rate a three or four. If views are all that is wanted, drive the Hansen Creek Road another mile for views that would rate a five or six. But views are not always what one needs for an outdoor experience. There are three choices for walks, with the first being the shortest.

Wanting to stretch my legs a bit, I drove I-90 to Exit 47. However, with sixty-eight cars at the Pratt Lake trailhead and seventy-one cars at the Lake Annette trailhead, I went looking for a trail to get away from so many people. I can't blame anyone for going to those lakes, for they are great destinations. I have boasted about these trails for years. But the parking lots prove my claim that there is a serious shortage of trails for the 290,000 day-hikers in our Cascade Mountains. Between lack of money, environmental laws, and the grizzly bear recovery zone, there is little hope of getting new trails in the next hundred years, thus the reason for this book: pointing out alternative roads-to-trails for hikers.

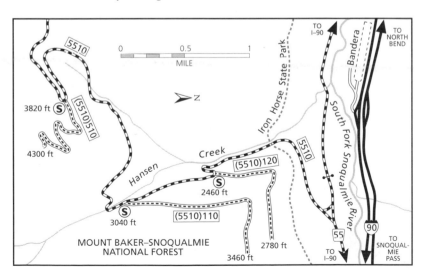

Driving directions: Drive I-90 to Exit 47. Go south, cross over the river, and in 0.3 mile, go right on the Tinkham Road, No. 55, signed "Hanson Creek." Drive another 1.3 miles and go left on the Hansen Creek Road 5510 (not signed).

Beargrass from Road 5510-510

ROAD 5510-120
Road status: Closed
Round trip: 3 miles
High point: 2800 feet
Elevation gain: 200

From the junction, drive 1.5 miles to a switchback and Road 5510-120, elevation 2460 feet, for the first of the three walks. While views are limited, solitude seems assured.

ROAD 5510-110
Road status: Gated
Round trip: 4 miles
High point: 3430 feet
Elevation gain: 600 feet

For the second walk, at 2.3 miles from the beginning of the Hanson Creek Road, find Road 5101-110 marked only by a rusty gate, elevation 2830 feet.

The Forest Service has abandoned these first two roads, but miners occasionally use them and keep them open, so the tread is good for hiking. Much of the way is walled by willows, hazels, and alders trying to take over the disturbed soil, and view windows are few. Not until the end of the road is there a good view spot. McClellan Butte to the west, Bandera and Granite Mountains across the valley, and the somewhat muted roar of I-90 far below.

ROAD 5510-510
Road status: Undecided
Round trip: 2 miles
High point: 4300 feet
Elevation gain: 450 feet

With unlimited views, this is my favorite. Drive on another 2-plus miles to Road 5510-510. It is still passable to four-wheel-drive vehicles. Park where the road gets steep, elevation 3820 feet. Except during hunting season, there is virtually no traffic along this route, so the walking is good and the views are great.

By Ira Spring

50 IRON HORSE TRAIL

Road status: Gated

RATTLESNAKE LAKE TO CASCADE CREST
One way: 21 miles
High point: 2400 feet
Elevation gain: 1500 feet
Open all year (west end), March–November (east end)

WASHINGTON CREEK
Round trip: 6 miles, allow 4 hours
High point: 1100 feet
Elevation gain: 130 feet
Open all year

WEST PORTAL OF CASCADE TUNNEL
Round trip: 5½ miles, allow 4 hours
High point: 2400 feet
Elevation gain: 200 feet
Open March–November

Maps: North Bend Ranger District and Green Trails: Nos. 206
Bandera, 207 Snoqualmie Pass

The Iron Horse Trail ain't what it was cracked up to be when first proposed. True, freight trains no longer disquiet the mountainside forest serenity; instead, deported to the freeway in the valley below, they toss family cars about in their wake like tumbleweeds in a dust devil. True, rails and ties no longer trip up careless feet and hooves; those impediments, as well as trees that so closely hedged the railroad as to make it a virtual tunnel through forest, have been removed to make a 40-foot-wide truck road and a 230-kilowatt powerline. (That buzz heard on a rainy day is not bees.)

So it's not really a "trail" at all, in the ancient and honorable definition. It's a "multi-use travelway." Among the "multis" are servicing trucks, which require a hard-surface road that tends to flatten feet. And no more trees close enough to reach out and touch in passing.

Another of the "multis" unexpected by dreamers of old is the new-fangled knobby-tired "mountain" bike. Well, we all love the bicycle. A fun machine, not loud, fumeless, and depleting no fossil fuels. And we all know how difficult it is to keep the wheels upright while going as slow as legs. Nevertheless, a pedestrian hardly can be expected to have a nice day when simians zip by his ear, sneering at siblings who can't move fast enough to escape the lions, nor can an equestrian when a Silent Menace spooks his steed. On the other hand, the biker who exults in creating a 20-knot wind is understandably aggravated by speedway-blocking clumps of chummy walkers. The answer is (ultimately) to separate the swifter (bikers, runners, skaters, truckers) from slower (walkers, wheelchairs, horses).

Lane separation, however, is needed only where traffic is heavy. For most of these 21 miles, hikers will not be much tempted by the naked swath where lightning buzzes in the wires overhead. Their destinations of choice will be the creeks, nigh onto a dozen major tumbles and countless trickles. Good intermediate accesses to the Iron Horse are Olallie State Park (walk west to Washington Creek, east to Change and Hall

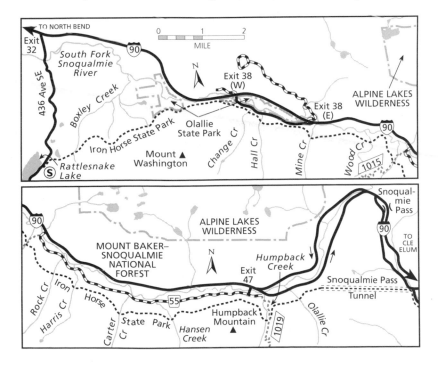

A trace of snow along the South Fork Snoqualmie River, from Iron Horse Trail

Creeks), and the McClellan Butte trail (walk east to Alice, Rock, Carter, and Hanson Creeks).

The two ends, though, are the pedestrian favorites, the west because low elevation keeps it open all year, and the east end because homesickness for our troglodyte ancestry draws us to holes in the ground.

Driving directions: For the western end, go off 1-90 on Exit 34 and turn south on 436 Avenue SE (Cedar Falls Road to Rattlesnake Lake), elevation 970 feet. (Until State Parks officially opens a trailhead here, use the temporary alternative: At ¼ mile short of the lake, go left on a wide gravel road. Park at the sharp bend. To the right, spot the barbwire fence along the watershed boundary, elevation 1000 feet. The trail follows the fence, skirting Christmas Lake to the powerline access road, which ascends to the Iron Horse Trail about 1 mile east of the eventual permanent trailhead.) The trail crosses Boxley Creek, rounds the slopes of Cedar Butte, and in 3 miles comes to the trestle over Washington Creek, 1100 feet, and grand views across the valley to Mount Si. And so home.

For the eastern end, go off 1-90 on Exit 47, turn right 0.1 mile, then go left on Road 55 for 0.6 mile to the Annette Lake trailhead, elevation 2200 feet. The trail crosses Humpback Creek and, at 1¼ miles, 2400 feet, intersects the Iron Horse to the west. At 2¾ miles, 2400 feet, is the west portal of the tunnel beneath the Cascade Crest. The east portal is 2¼ miles more at Hyak. Check your flashlight batteries. Beware of cave bears and things that go bump.

By Harvey Manning

51 CCC ROAD

Road status: Gated
Round trip: 18 miles, or shorter portions
High point: 1520 feet
Elevation gain: 600 feet, loss 600 feet

Maps: Green Trails: Nos. 206 Bandera, 174 Mount Si

The CCC Road starts just around the corner from the busy Mount Si trail, climbs above the South Fork Snoqualmie valley, and turns north into the Middle Fork Snoqualmie valley. I first heard about it in the late 1980s, and have enjoyed it since as a spectacular motor-free route into the Middle Fork. Views start early and rarely stop, as the road winds under the slopes of Teneriffe, Green, and Bessemer.

Driving directions: Drive the Mount Si Road past the Mount Si trailhead to the end of the pavement. There is no parking allowed beyond here, so find a safe place to park and begin your hike or bike ride. Ignore the "Road Closed" signs (it's not), and climb the steep gravel road nearly one mile to the CCC Road gate, elevation 1272 feet.

From the gate, the road continues up the flat-topped moraine that forms the southeast shoulder of Mount Teneriffe. When I reach the top, I always look north up a short spur road for a bit of Middle Fork culture: A 1950s vintage Chevy sitting atop a giant stump. (How it got there, no one seems to know.) Then it's time for a swig of water and a look at Mount Washington, Defiance, and other South Fork peaks. After taking my fill of South Fork views, I begin my journey up the CCC Road high above the Middle Fork valley.

The road/trail follows the flat edge of the moraine for a long mile, and then begins its traverse along the base of Green Mountain. Soon it reaches my favorite rest spot, a viewpoint where the road cuts across a granite cliff. I sit at the edge and gaze across the valley at the towers of Russian Butte. South of Russian Butte are the steep slopes of Zorro Ridge, named for the eroding logging road that once zigzagged across its face.

Although scars remain, Mountains to Sound Greenway crews did a fine job of decommissioning and replanting the road (another future trail possibility).

For the next few miles the road tunnels through second- and third-growth forest. If it's October, I search for chanterelles, but although conditions usually look perfect, I never find more than a few.

About 5 miles from the gate, the road crosses Big Blowout Creek, a shin-high ford most of the year. After Big Blowout, the CCC joins the Bessemer road. In another ⅓ mile, the roads separate as the Bessemer road veers uphill and the CCC Road heads to the right.

Now comes my favorite part of the route. Long abandoned as a road, the remaining 2½ miles are the best demonstration of a road-to-trail project in the region—and Mother Nature did all the work. Alders, salmonberries, and wildflowers have converged on the road, converting it to a narrow trail covered by needles and other forest debris. In the spring, adjacent ponds swarm with polliwogs, and from a mossy cliff are views of the meandering Middle Fork, Garfield's granite walls, and the roadless Pratt River valley. A normally laconic friend, newly introduced to this trail, said over and over, "This is delightful. I never use that word, but this is delightful."

As the CCC Road nears its end at the Middle Fork road, it crosses a big washout. I hop the big boulders and follow a boot-built trail to the

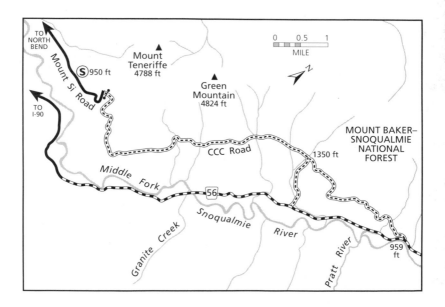

road again, which soon drops to the Middle Fork road 56.

Spurred by community interest in a CCC trail, the Forest Service will soon extend the route 3 miles to the Taylor River area. They've surveyed the route and construction starts soon, with completion likely by 2002. The new route combines new trail with sections of old logging roads.

By Mark Boyer

Mount Garfield from CCC Road

52 GREEN MOUNTAIN

Road status: Gated
Round trip: 12 miles, allow 5 hours
High point: 4300 feet
Elevation gain: Up to 3500 feet

Map: Green Trails: No. 174 Mount Si

Green Mountain is a hidden gem located between Mount Teneriffe and Bessemer Mountain. With wild roads that can be converted to trails and wilder open areas that can be made into trails, this is one of the greatest untapped resources in the Middle Fork Snoqualmie River valley.

Access is difficult. There is very limited parking at the gate. The actual allocated space for cars is almost a mile downvalley at the Mount Teneriffe trailhead. From that point it is still another 3½ miles along the

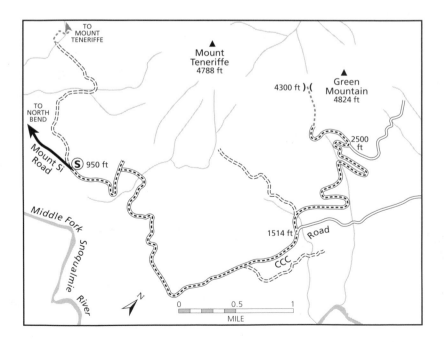

Tom Kirkendall and the Middle Fork Snoqualmie River, from Green Mountain (photo by Vicky Spring)

old CCC Road to the base of Green Mountain. The alternative is to bicycle to the base and find a place to stash the wheels before heading up.

Driving directions: Drive I-90 to North Bend. Drive into town, then go right on North Bend Way. Head east, passing the North Bend Forest Service office, to Mount Si Road (also signed "432 SE"). Cross the Middle Fork Snoqualmie River and continue straight ahead for 3.6 miles to find the Mount Teneriffe trailhead on the left, elevation 950 feet.

Your route continues on up the now steeply climbing Mount Si Road, past the "Road Closed—Do Not Enter" signs. Stay with the main road, which makes a sweeping turn before reaching a locked gate at 1300 feet.

The road continues climbing, heading up to the top of an old terminal moraine, strip-logged and now very brushy. You will pass several side-roads, but the main route is generally clear. At the crest of the moraine is a four-way intersection. Go straight. At one point the road divides; stay left and head out to open views that extend over Teneriffe, Green, and Bessemer, as well as the vertical mass of Garfield.

By Vicky Spring

53 GRANITE CREEK ROAD

Road status: Gated
Round trip: 11 miles, allow 5 hours
High point: 3100 feet
Elevation gain: 2300 feet

Map: Green Trails: No. 206 Bandera

What a difference a gate can make!

My first experience with the Granite Creek Road was in a car. We did not stay long. It was a noisy place, with jeeps, fat-tired trucks, motorcycles, off-road vehicles, and an assortment of family cars attempting to be off-road vehicles, all grinding their way up and down the steep grade as fast as they could shift gears. The destination for most of these visitors was the old Thompson Lake trailhead, which was then an easy one-mile hike in the wilderness. Avoiding the beer drinking, radio-toting crowd, we branched off to Granite Lakes and found them in a tangle of brush, nearly inaccessible to all but the most determined jungle explorers.

Fifteen years later we revisited Granite Creek Road. With a sturdy gate to ensure peace from the start, we discovered beautiful forests, a cascading creek, excellent scenery, a couple of good-looking lakes, and plenty of solitude.

Driving directions: Leave Interstate 90 at Exit 34, signed "468th Avenue SE," and head north past the Seattle East Auto Truck Plaza to the Middle Fork Road (No. 56). Turn right and continue on until the road splits. Take either the Lake Dorothy or the Middle Fork Road; the two will rejoin in 2.1 miles. Once back together, follow the Middle Fork Road upvalley another 0.2 mile to pavement's end. On the right is a parking area and the start of the route up Mailbox Peak. Park here, elevation 820 feet.

▲

The hike begins with a 0.3-mile walk up the Middle Fork Road or, when it is built, on a trail that will parallel the road. When you reach a major logging road heading uphill, go right. After crossing a clearing, the road heads through a stately, second-growth forest. This is a fascinating area, with 100-year-old Douglas firs growing out of giant old stumps, with springboard notches made by loggers using handsaws. The road is lined with spinally, moss-hung maples, and the forest floor is covered with ferns.

After a pleasant mile, the road leaves the forest and heads steeply up into a massive, brush-covered clearcut. Soft tread is replaced with lots of rocks underfoot. The road heads up at a steady pace, switchbacking across the hillside. Spur roads are passed, but the main route is obvious. A grove of trees and a short descent to cross an unnamed creek offer welcome breaks in the monotony of the climb.

Beyond the clearcut, the road levels and traverses a cliff. Near the 2-mile point, there is a sudden sharp bend into the Granite Creek drainage. A short ¼ mile beyond, the road crosses to the east side of the creek, then parallels it on its steep, then steeper, then steeper still route up the narrow drainage.

The next landmark is a quick switchback. A short ½ mile beyond, a spur road branches off on the right. In 1999, this road was undergoing rehabilitation to return it to a more natural state, so it is uncertain what this intersection will look like in the future.

Continue on up Granite Creek Road for another ¼ mile, then go right on a spur road, which was also undergoing rehab procedures in 1999. In the first 100 yards, cross two creeks that could use bridges now that the culverts are gone. This is also the best campsite in the area.

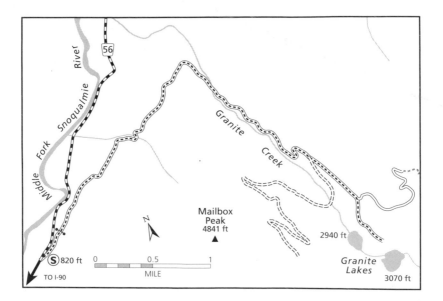

Beargrass and upper Granite Lake (photo by Vicky Spring)

The road descends, becoming more of a boulder field then an actual vehicle passageway. After ¼ mile, reach an old logging platform. Look over the side for a trail descending to the lower Granite Lake. If the upper lake is your goal, continue down to the end of the old roadbed, then bushwhack your way up using the creek as a guide.

If Thompson Lake is your objective, continue up the main road another 1½ miles, passing two spur roads on the left. The trail is long abandoned and likely to be very brushy.

By Vicky Spring

54 SOUTH BESSEMER MOUNTAIN

Road status: Gated
Round trip: 12 miles to summit
High point: 5000 feet
Elevation gain: 4000 feet

Map: Green Trails: No. 174 Mount Si

In the manner of logging roads, the Bessemer Road is not one road but many, an identifiable main trunk with four or five spurs of note. It intersects the old CCC Road about a mile from its starting point on the Middle Fork Road, joins it for about a half mile, and then heads uphill in a series of gradually steepening switchbacks. The main trunk reaches the crest of the Green–Bessemer ridge in about 5 miles. The road is gated; this keeps out sport utilities but not the occasional ATV or dirt bike.

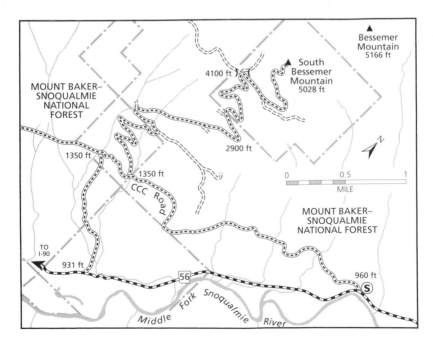

Driving directions: Drive the Middle Fork Road (No. 56) 5 miles from where the pavement ends. Park below the gate, just off the Middle Fork Road, elevation 960 feet.

I have always liked the first mile of the road, a walk along the valley bottom. There are some residual big trees in the first half mile: old limby Sitka spruces and gnarled, mossy bigleaf maple on the north side of the road, and a couple big red-cedars a hundred yards or so south of the road. This stretch seldom gets persistent snow cover. In winter or spring, when the leaves are off the alders, the views are better, the valley-bottom brush is less dense, and the moss on the trees is a vivid green.

A handful of years ago I saw a cougar and her yearling cub on the stretch of road where the Bessemer and CCC Roads coincide. I was alone, jogging, which is said to be a good way to give a cougar ideas that you might be worth eating. I did a lot of looking-behind-me that day.

The first 2000 feet of climbing after the Bessemer Road branches off uphill from the CCC Road are through fifty-year-old second growth. This natural hemlock regeneration is a very dark, close-canopied forest with virtually no shrub or herb layer growing on the forest floor. As a hike it feels flat, tiresomely flat, going up or down. "I came out here to climb this darn mountain, not traverse back and forth across it," you say to yourself. The case is altered on a bicycle. On a bike, it feels like a sustained climb that never backs off enough to let you recover fully. It just keeps climbing and climbing and climbing until you are about ready to fall off the bike and die.

The first respectable view out over the valley comes at around 2900 feet, at the end of a long switchback grade. Not a bad choice for a turnaround spot if you are on a bike or doing an early season hike.

The upper mountain feels different than the lower. The logging is more recent and, because of the steep terrain and the harsher growing conditions, has wrought some terrible damage. Regeneration failures and small trees mean extensive views, though. And a closeup view of the consequences of unrestrained industrial logging is always instructive.

About ⅓ mile beyond the first good lookout, the road forks and the notion of a "main trunk route" gets a little vague. The right-turning branch offers the most direct climbing route, reaching the ridge top in about ¾ of a mile. Unless you are a superman (I am not), you will not be able to ride that way; you can continue straight ahead for a longer, more gradual, yet still taxing route to the ridge crest.

Bessemer Mountain on an early spring walk

Reaching the ridge top around 4100 feet at "Kiss-your-ass-goodbye" Pass, so named by the unfortunates who drove logging trucks on this road, you have three choices. The left-hand route traverses the ridge for a mile before stopping abruptly at a log landing. The route straight ahead actually doesn't go that far anymore, but it's quite interesting; the construction of the road destabilized the slope to the degree that a huge section of it peeled off the mountain, leaving a sheer cliff where logging trucks once hauled out loads of mountain hemlock. The right-hand route takes you to the summit of South Bessemer in another mile and a thousand feet of climbing.

The view from South Bessemer is a grand view of logging devastation. West and south, the view is generally stark. To the north, the craggy summit ridge of Bessemer Mountain is visible less than a mile off. The distance is short, but the travel is hard: The true summit of Bessemer is one of the Middle Fork's least-visited summits. To the east, the sweeping view over the Middle Fork valley and on to the summits of the Cascade Crest is a compensation for the ugliness elsewhere.

By Kevin Geraghty

55 ROAD 5640
QUARTZ CREEK

Road status: Gated
Round trip: 10 miles, allow 7 hours
High point: 3198 feet
Elevation gain: 2000 feet

Maps: North Bend Ranger District and Green Trails: No. 174
Mount Si

An impressive view of the Cathedral-like towers of Mount Garfield. Although the road is firmly gated, the first 2½ miles is drivable, but without traffic it is a very agreeable walk. Best in the spring when the way is lined with bright yellow violets.

Driving directions: Drive Interstate 90 east from North Bend to Exit 34, go off north on 468 Avenue SE, and, 0.4 mile past Truck Town, turn right on SE Middle Fork (Snoqualmie River) Road 56. Pass the Gateway parking at 11.8 miles, at 12 miles cross the Taylor River, and, at the Y just beyond, go left on the Taylor River road (Road 5640). In 0.5 mile is a second bridge, firmly gated, over the river. Park here, elevation 1150 feet.

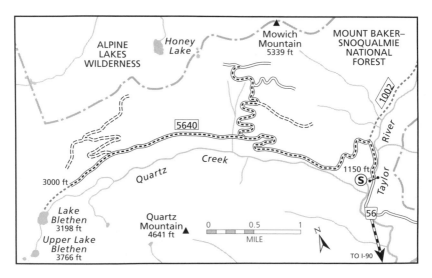

The Quartz Creek road/trail

Walk the Taylor River road/trail a third of a mile to a Y. The Quartz Creek road/trail goes off left and heads steeply up in cool forest. At 2 miles the road makes a sharp switchback, with a view up the valley and back to the towers on Garfield. At 2½ miles is the first of two washouts that best be crossed later in the summer. For bigger views, go right on a sideroad/trail and follow it steeply toward the 5339-foot summit of Mowich Mountain.

The main road/trail up Quartz Creek peters out at about 3000 feet, and the path beaten by fisherman feet finishes the ½ mile to Lake Blethen, 3198 feet, a pleasant little lake surrounded by trees and cliffs. There are a couple of campsites, but, unfortunately, the lakeshore is privately owned and the owner is threatening to build on it.

By Ira Spring

56

ROAD 5640-101
TAYLOR RIVER

OTTER FALLS AND LIPSY LAKE

Road status: Closed
Round trip: 8½ miles, allow 4 hours
High point: 1750 feet
Elevation gain: 650 feet

Maps: North Bend Ranger District and Green Trails: Nos. 174
   Mount Si, 175 Skykomish

The first time I saw Otter Falls and little Lipsy Lake was from my car window. The Lake Dorothy road was under construction. It was to be a scenic drive up the Taylor River, past Snoqualmie Lake, down to Lake Dorothy, and out US Highway 2. Although there is still a road sign pointing to Lake Dorothy, there were enough green-bonded people to stop the road to the lake, which is now in the Alpine Lakes Wilderness.

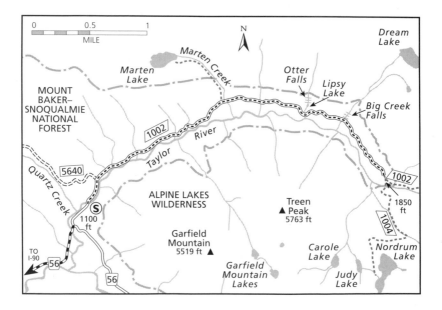

Otter Falls and Lipsy Lake

While the road sign still points to Lake Dorothy, the road builders have given up, and the Taylor River road has become a delightful foot trail through green forest. The river is always within sound, and the many sharp peaks of Garfield Mountain can sometimes be seen above the treetops.

Doing research for a new hikes book, by foot I went back to Otter Falls, but in the ensuing twenty-five years, trees have grown up and are now hiding the falls. I walked 6 miles before I realized I had gone too far. At home, poring over my maps, I found my mistake. Even so, on my second try I still had a problem finding the exact place to leave the trail, and ended up pushing through a dense jungle of slide alder.

Driving directions: Drive Interstate 90 east from North Bend to Exit 34, go off north on 468 Avenue SE, and, 0.4 mile past Truck Town, turn right on SE Middle Fork (Snoqualmie River) Road 56. Pass the Gateway parking at 11.8 miles, at 12 miles cross the Taylor River, and, at the Y just beyond, go left on the Taylor River road. In 0.5 mile is a second bridge, firmly gated, over the river. Park here, elevation 1100 feet.

Walk the Taylor River road/trail a third of a mile to a Y. Where Quartz Creek goes left, go right. At 3 miles is the first of the big waters, Marten Creek, the falls churning a pool of limeade. Harvey Manning claims that, just short of Marten Creek, a boot path leads to awesome ancient cedars, some more than 12 feet in diameter.

Marten Creek is crossed on a rotten bridge that may soon be replaced. In the next mile, several loud creeks tumble through culverts. There is also a rockslide that must be carefully crossed, and jackstraw jumbles of avalanched logs where passage has been made possible by a lot of chainsawing.

At 1¼ miles from Marten Creek is Otter Creek, flowing through a particularly large culvert. Don't make my mistake and start up too soon; go several hundred feet beyond Otter Creek and find a distinct though unsigned trail climbing through a moss-covered forest floor. Lipsy Lake! A gem of a pool below a 500-foot granite slab, down which Otter Creek plunges in one waterfall after another.

Beyond Otter Creek another ¾ mile is Big Creek, 1700 feet, crossed by a massive concrete bridge, a reminder of the Lake Dorothy Highway.

For a person wanting more exercise, Snoqualmie Lake is a couple of long, steep miles away, at 3470 feet in the Alpine Lakes Wilderness.

By Ira Spring

57 Dirty Harry's

Road status: Closed

TO DIRTY HARRY'S BALCONY
Round trip: 3 miles
High point: 2663 feet
Elevation gain: 1300 feet

TO DIRTY HARRY'S PEAK
Round trip: 5 miles
High point: 4700 feet
Elevation gain: 3300 feet

Maps: North Bend Ranger District and Green Trails: No. 206
(road not shown)

There was a lot of variety along this road/trail, because it is so steep and passes through different vegetation zones. It's rocky like an old-fashioned road bed in the lower parts; there are some dry, hard-packed parts; there are some meadow parts; there are definitely some creek bed parts; there are many mossy, emerald green parts; there's a thick, pale green-blue lichen part; etcetera, etcetera. There's also a sizeable rockslide at about 3400 feet that requires some rock-stepping. The variety helps take your mind off the steady steepness.

Driving directions: Coming from the west, go off I-90 at Exit 38 and drive old US Highway 10, now a rest-and-recreation boulevard that ends in 2 miles at the eastbound Exit 38. Follow signs marked "Fire Training Academe." Go under I-90 0.2 mile to a gate, signed "Locked after 4 p.m. Road ends 2.5 miles ahead." At 0.2 mile from the gate is a bridge over the South Fork Snoqualmie. In 0.4 mile more, on a curve and easy to miss, Dirty Harry's Logging Road, unsigned, climbs to the right. Just a trail now. And creek bed. Elevation 1350 feet.

First, somebody's been maintaining and clearing the trail. The rock bed is fairly clear of brush, but is moderately eroded. When I was there, shrubs previously growing in the trail had been lopped off at ground level, all the way to the mountaintop. Somebody did one heck of a job clearing it, and occasional maintenance is needed just to keep it from disappearing again.

Second, the trail goes clear to the top of the mountain. There are sure to be good views northeast down to Granite Lakes and south down to the highway and across to Mount Washington, McClellan Butte, and Mount Kent, but the Sunday I went the clouds never broke up. It snowed steadily from about 10 minutes after I got to the top.

Third, parts of the trail are pretty steep (steep enough so that rocks roll downhill when you stumble or slip), but at the same time, the trail is always wide enough and has a smooth grade. Steep, but steady. There isn't any scrambling (except for the rockslide; see below).

About 1½ miles up, there is a well-marked (with pink plastic) side trail out to a steep, exposed Dirty Harry's Balcony cliff-top viewpoint over I-90, elevation 2613 feet. It takes about 10 minutes to walk out to the viewpoint, through a thick, deep, dark cedar forest. The viewpoint is exposed and (I suppose) plenty dangerous. This is not the place to take young children. If one slipped off the small view-perch, one might not survive. But it is a nice place to sit and eat a sandwich. The trail to the

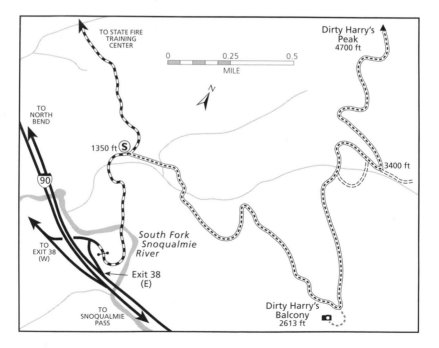

I-90 and the South Fork Snoqualmie River valley, from Dirty Harry's Balcony

viewpoint, again, is very well marked with frequent pink plastic ribbons and is a good introduction to off-trail exploration.

Not too much wildlife along the trail. Lots of birds, however. I saw one round-eyed rabbit at the top. And two poops of black bear (I think) in the middle of the trail. There was still some lingering snow on the summit, especially around the bases of the 3- to 4-foot-diameter tree stumps. Whoever cleared the trail also seems to have cleared a couple of side trails. Off of this short spur trail there are two other well-marked trails, one leading generally northeast from the viewpoint trail, the other going generally southeast from there. I didn't follow either of these for more than 100 yards. They both were brushed (but narrow) and well marked with frequent pink plastic markers. Closer toward the top, I think there was another spur trail leading to the west, possibly another access to the top or access to the ridge top heading northwest; and I think there was a spur trail at the ridge top saddle, leading to the easterly summit at elevation 4700 feet.

By Steve Bernheim

58 ROAD 70
GREENWATER RIVER

Road status: Closed
Round trip: 4½ miles
High point: 2400 feet
Elevation gain: 300 feet

Maps: White River Ranger District and Green Trails: No. 239
Lester

A massive washout a few years ago led the Forest Service to relocate this stretch of road higher on the slope. The old roadbed, however, is still hikable and offers river access to hikers, anglers, and elk alike.

Driving directions: From the ranger station in Enumclaw, drive Highway 410 east 19.7 miles (through the hamlet of Greenwater) and turn left on FS Road 70. Drive 4.7 miles, then angle off on the gravel road to the left as the paved road turns sharply right and starts to climb away from the river. This gravel road ends shortly at a massive tank trap and is the southern trailhead for this hike, elevation 2100 feet.

The first several hundred yards have the litter and shell casings found at any site within easy reach of the road, and occasional gunfire can be

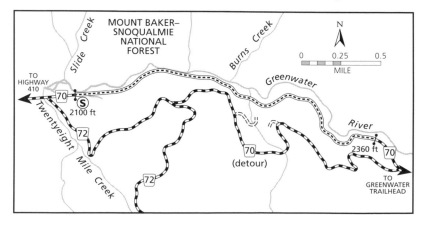

Greenwater River

heard from the gravel pit up the slope on Road 72. However, these are replaced within a few minutes of walking by lupine, daisies, clover, and the sound of the rushing river below. The first half mile of trail offers access to the riverbank at half a dozen places, with obvious good camp-sites. Abundant elk tracks prove that the road still sees some quiet traffic, but no revving motors or ORV tracks despoil the way. At 1 mile the first of two huge water ditches are crossed, both nearly 40 feet deep and of-fering just a bit of scrambling to liven up an otherwise sedate hike.

The river remains sporadically in view for the rest of the hike, but no more easy access presents itself as the trail gently climbs up the steep wall of the valley. The opposite slope of the river valley is logged in places, but enough tall trees are standing at river's edge to provide decent raptor habitat. At 1¾ miles the washout that closed down the works is visible. Gravity vetoed further vehicle traffic, and small chunks of pave-ment, painted with lines, are still visible 75 feet downslope. A trail uphill of the slide allows those on foot easy passage. At 2¼ miles you reach pavement again, as FS Road 70 picks up again where it left off (8¼ miles total from Highway 410, elevation 2360 feet).

By Jim Walke

59 ROADS 7224 AND 7226
GEORGE CREEK HILL

Road status: Proposed to be closed

Maps: White River Ranger District and Green Trails: No. 239 Lester

ROAD 7224
Round trip: 8 miles
High point: 4800 feet
Elevation gain: 1250 feet

A high-level overview of a Western tree farm caps this road walk that commands fine valley views along almost its entire length.

Driving directions: From the ranger station in Enumclaw, drive Highway 410 east 19.7 miles (2 miles beyond the hamlet of Greenwater) and turn left on FS Road 70. Drive 5.9 miles and turn right on unpaved FS Road 72. At 0.7 mile from Road 70, turn left on Road 7220 (farthest left of three choices), at 1.8 miles stay straight on Road 7220, and at 4 miles

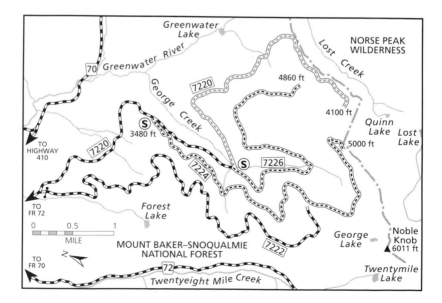

from Road 70, stop at the juncture of Road 7220 (left) and No. 7224 (right). All junctions were signed at the time of this writing.

▲▲

Road 7224 is barely blocked by two 18-foot gravel mounds, and it obviously still receives a bit of traffic from high-clearance vehicles. The fact, however, that we saw no one else on a fine July weekend overnight trip should tell you something about the level of vehicular traffic. As a matter of fact, from the quantity of fresh signs we saw, I would say that you have a much better chance of spotting elk than any cars on this road.

The tread is level and smooth, and the slope climbs gently due south at first. The views of the valley containing George Creek are good, but they get better. At 3 miles the trail begins to swing to the east at the head of the valley, and the views stretch down to the junction with the Greenwater River valley. The arms of the valley frame a landscape checkered by logged areas and framed by roads, but it's still remarkable in sheer size and scale.

At 3½ miles is a great view of 6011-foot Noble Knob, which marks a corner of the Norse Peak Wilderness. At 4 miles the trail enters a mildly

Hiking in the clouds on Road 7224

boggy plateau, which helps send George Creek on its way, one of several water sources along the hike. The climax view of this hike, including Baker and Glacier Peak, is found just short of this plateau. The road continues for another mile almost due north and climbs to 5000 feet, but it ends on a logged ridge with no more views.

ROAD 7226
Round trip: 7.2 miles
High point: 4800 feet
Elevation gain: 1300 feet

Views of the Greenwater River valley highlight this barely abandoned road.

Driving directions: From the ranger station in Enumclaw, drive US Highway 410 east 19.7 miles (through the hamlet of Greenwater) and turn left on FS Road 70. Drive 5.9 miles and turn right on unpaved FS Road 72.

At 0.7 mile from Road 70, turn left on Road 7220 (farthest left of three choices), at 1.8 miles stay straight on Road 7220, at 4 miles stay left on Road 7220, and, finally, at 5.4 miles from FS Road 70, turn right on Road 7226. All junctions were signed at the time of this writing.

At the time of this writing, Road 7226 was still drivable for much of its length. Although it obviously no longer receives official attention, users who happen to have a chainsaw and peavey in the back of the truck are keeping it open. Deadfalls are moved or cut (one large tree blocked the road at 2.6 miles on my first visit, but was neatly cut and moved a week later when I returned), and narrow paths are clear through some minor rockfall. Drive until your nerve fails you, then park and start hiking.

Winding through forest for much of its length, at 1¼ miles the road crosses burbling George Creek, the last reliable water source for this hike. Soon thereafter the road swings to the north, climbing a bit more steeply (steep for a road, still easy for a hiker). At 2.4 miles, the road turns again to the south, and views of the Greenwater River Valley open up to the north. Logging activity is evident at road's end (4860 feet) but the painfully new growth equals views. At least it should, but I was in a cloud at the time and could only see a few feet. (Mine, I think . . .) From the map, the views should include the Norse Peak Wilderness, miles of the Greenwater River Valley, and the Maggie Creek drainage to the east. Cleared spots on top testify as to the quality of the camping.

By Jim Walke

60 NACHES WAGON ROAD OF 1853

Road status: Open to ORVs

TO "THE CLIFF"
Round trip: 1 mile
High point: 3300 feet
Elevation gain: 800 feet

TO NACHES PASS
Round trip: 10 miles
High point: 4800 feet
Elevation gain: 2300 feet

Maps: White River Ranger District and Green Trails: No. 239
Lester (trail not shown)

This should be the most famous road-to-trail in the country. Unfortunately, the wagon tracks have been ground away by thousands of offroad vehicles.

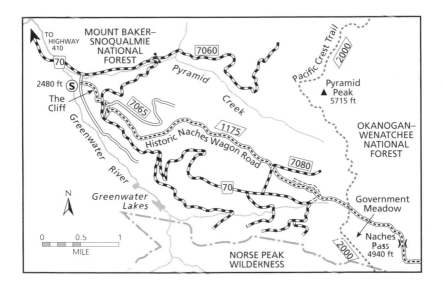

West end of the old Naches Wagon Road

In 1853, the first train of thirty-six wagons crossed the Cascade Mountains on an old Indian path. From Yakima, they went over Naches Pass and down into the Greenwater River watershed. Making the foot and horse trail wide enough for the wagons was bad enough, but on the west side there was "The Cliff"—a drop of over 800 feet in a little over ½ mile. Using rope and leather straps, one by one each wagon was lowered. On the west side they found the Greenwater valley a jungle of giant trees and brush. Only one other wagon train followed, and, except for farmers driving cattle to west-side markets, the route was abandoned until 1910, when the government reopened the road for a horse patrol.

In 1953, to celebrate the one hundredth anniversary of the first crossing, a radio personality organized a group of jeep riders to widen the path and cross the pass. The publicity opened a floodgate, and ever since then it has been a popular off-road vehicle spot that has destroyed most of the evidence of the first crossing, and deeply eroded the track.

I first walked the road in 1969 with four Forest Rangers who were assessing the route for possible inclusion in the National Historic Register. Richard Simmons, the Naches District Ranger, and the retired Ranger Nevan McCullough wanted to bar the ORVs and have the wagon road added to the register. The other two, from the regional office, said that too much damage had already been done, and the checkerboard ownership would make it too difficult to manage. While hiking, Nevan explained that the top-heavy wagons stayed on the ridge top instead of contouring around a steep hillside, while the jeeps had opened portions of their route on the hillside. Going over each high point along the way, he pointed out the wagon route and axe cuts.

For hikers, all is not lost. Although cut by two logging roads, the first ½ mile to the middle of "The Cliff" is closed to machines and the whole trail system is closed to motors between November 15 and July 15.

Driving directions: Take Highway 410 east from Enumclaw 2 miles past the hamlet of Greenwater. Go left on FS Road 70. In about 9 miles, cross the Greenwater bridge, and in 0.4 mile, go right on a short spur road to the Greenwater trailhead. Just short of the large trailhead find the Naches Trail No. 1175.

▲▲

The trail starts out on a reasonable grade. As you walk, visualize the trail as it was in 1853, before the dirt eroded away from the big rocks. Look for old blazes that marked the way. As the way climbs, find parts of the 1910 Government Trail that switchbacked up the steeper sections. In a short ½ mile cross Road 70 and keep going higher. At a long ½ mile from the start, reach Road 7065 and the end of motor-free travail. Off-road vehicles are no longer allowed on the steepest part of "The Cliff," where they had once used cables to lower their vehicles, as the pioneers had done with rope and straps. The motor trail is well off to the side and is so steep and so deeply trenched, hiking it would be miserable.

Directional sign on a 100-year-old blaze

Tributary logging roads from Road 70 cross the Naches Trail several times. Drive Road 70 some 2 miles beyond the Greenwater River bridge, to the first crossing described above. A bit farther is Road 7065, also described. At milepost 14 an unsigned road goes left, splits, and both branches cross the trail. At 0.8 mile beyond milepost 15, another unsigned road crosses the trail only 2 miles from Naches Pass.

By Ira Spring

61 ROAD 7530-410 LONESOME LAKE VIEW

Road status: Open to high-clearance vehicles
Round trip: 2 or 4 miles
High points: 5400 feet or 5700 feet
Elevation gains: 950 feet or 1250 feet

Maps: White River Ranger District and Green Trails: No. 238
  Greenwater

Lonesome Lake is no longer lonesome, as it gets 3000 visits a year. An abandoned logging road that leads from the lake is still useable to four-wheel-drive vehicles, but there is so little traffic it makes pleasant walking.

Driving directions: Drive Highway 410 east from Enumclaw, pass the town of Greenwater, and, between mileposts 46 and 47, turn right on paved West Fork White River Forest Road 74 and drive 0.5 mile to a Y.

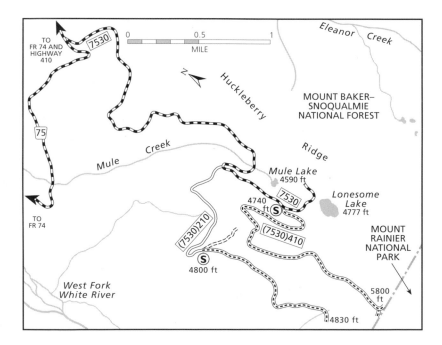

Both roads point to Haller Pass (a loop), but the lower road also points to Lonesome Lake. Part of the way is paved. At 6.2 miles from Highway 410, go left on Road 75 (not signed at time of research), leaving the pavement and climbing. At 9.7 miles from the highway, go right on Road 7530 and drive another 3.6 miles to Lonesome Lake.

Walk around the lake, and then drive back 0.1 mile to Road 7530-410, elevation 4740 feet.

The first 300 or 400 feet have been ditched and cross-ditched, but that is nothing to four-wheelers and their big fat tires. Beyond this obstacle the road is smooth walking. In a long ¼ mile, Mount Baker, Glacier Peak, and Mount Stewart rise above the foothills. In a short mile Mount Rainier comes in view. Find a log to sit on it, dig out the peanut butter and crackers. I am happy to just sit and look at The Mountain, but Pat has to see how far the road goes, so on we go. A bit farther we look down at people fishing in Lonesome Lake. The way enters a cool forest, then in 2 miles breaks out in a large clearcut right on the national park boundary.

Mount Rainier seems close enough to touch. Certainly if one is lucky, one could watch and maybe hear avalanches roar over Willis Wall. Take a Rainier map and identify all the features before you.

By Ira Spring

Mount Rainier from Road 7530-410

62 ROADS 7300-227 AND 7500-226
HUCKLEBERRY RIDGE

ROAD 7300-227
Road status: Closed
Round trip: 1 mile
High point: 4400 feet
Elevation gain: none

ROAD 7500-226
Road status: To be closed
Round trip: 1 mile
High point: 4796 feet
Elevation gain: 145 feet

Maps: White River Ranger District and Green Trails: No. 238
Greenwater

Two of the grandest views and flower-lined roads in the Mount Rainier area. But there is a fly in the ointment: One road has been so thoroughly put to bed that it is virtually impossible to hike, and the other road has not yet been closed off to vehicles.

Although there are three roads to Huckleberry Ridge, we chose the West Fork White River Road, because the first 6.5 miles are paved.

Driving directions: Drive Highway 410 east from Enumclaw, pass the town of Greenwater, and, between mileposts 46 and 47, turn right on paved Forest Road 74 and drive 0.5 mile to a Y. Both roads point to Haller Pass. Because part of the way is paved, we went straight ahead, on the West Fork road. At 6.2 miles from the 410 highway, go left on Road 75 (not signed at time of research), leaving the pavement and climbing. At 9.7 miles from the highway, pass Road 7530 to Lonesome Lake and, at 10.2 miles, reach a junction with Road 73 and a choice of the two roads/trails.

I suggest hiking both. So go right 0.7 mile to a saddle. Go left a few hundred feet to where Road 7300-227 is blocked, elevation 4380 feet.

In early August the abandoned road was knee-deep in yellow asters and vetch, with patches of lupine and paintbrush and an unforgettable view of Rainier. We scrambled over the tank trap that blocked the road and the way looked easy. It wasn't, for the roadbed had been torn up. Pits and ankle-twisting boulders were hidden in the flowers, making this a beautiful but treacherous walk.

We had looked forward to walking 1½ miles to its end, but had to give up in a short ½ mile. We don't recommend going farther.

Flower-lined Huckleberry Ridge Road 7500-226, with massive Mount Rainier in the background

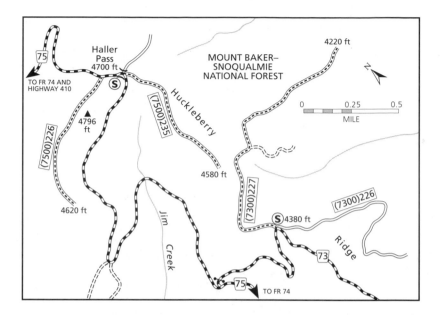

The day was young and we wanted something better. We drove back to Road 75 and followed it 2.2 miles to Haller Pass, elevation 4700 feet (12.4 miles from Highway 410).

On the west side of Haller Pass is Road 7500-226, abandoned but still drivable in a high-clearance family car. You may wish to park at the pass and walk the ½ mile on the road, lined with asters, paintbrush, and lupine, to an unobstructed, 4796-foot viewpoint of Rainier. From this angle, the Winthrop Glacier and Willis Wall dominate.

By Ira Spring

INDEX

Available at fine bookstores and outdoor stores, by phone at (800) 553-4453, or on the Web at www.mountaineersbooks.org

Hidden Hikes in Western Washington by Karen Sykes. $16.95 paperback. 0-89886-859-9.

Exploring Washington's Wild Areas: A Guide for Hikers, Backpackers, Climbers, Cross-Country Skiers, and Paddlers, 2nd Edition by Marge and Ted Mueller. $18.95 paperback. 0-89886-807-6.

100 Classic Hikes in™ Washington by Ira Spring and Harvey Manning. $19.95 paperback. 0-89886-586-7.

Hiking Washington's Geology by Scott Babcock and Robert Carson. $16.95 paperback. 0-89886-548-4.

100 Classic Backcountry Ski and Snowboard Routes in Washington by Rainer Burgdorfer. $17.95 paperback. 0-89886-661-8.

Snowshoe Routes: Washington by Dan Nelson. $16.95 paperback. 0-89886-585-9.

50 Trail Runs in Washington by Cheri Pompeo Gillis. $16.95 paperback. 0-89886-715-0.

Animal Tracks of the Pacific Northwest by Karen Pandell and Chris Stall. $6.95 paperback. 0-89886-012-1.

Northwest Trees by Stephen F. Arno and Ramona P. Hammerly. $14.95 paperback. 0-916890-50-3.

Northwest Mountain Weather: Understanding and Forecasting for the Backcountry User by Jeff Renner. $10.95 paperback. 0-89886-297-3.

Staying Found: The Complete Map & Compass Handbook, 3rd Edition by June Fleming. $12.95 paperback. 0-89886-785-1.

GPS Made Easy: Using Global Positioning Systems in the Outdoors, 3rd Edition by Lawrence Letham. $14.95 paperback. 0-89886-802-5.

First Aid: A Pocket Guide, 4th Edition by Christopher Van Tilburg, M.D. $3.50 paperback. 0-89886-719-3.

Emergency Survival: A Pocket Guide by Christopher Van Tilburg, M.D. $3.50 paperback. 0-89886-768-1.

Wilderness 911: A Step-By-Step Guide for Medical Emergencies and Improvised Care in the Backcountry by Eric A. Weiss, M.D. $16.95 paperback. 0-89886-597-2.

Everyday Wisdom: 1001 Expert Tips for Hikers by Karen Berger. $16.95 paperback. 0-89886-523-9.

THE MOUNTAINEERS, founded in 1906, is a nonprofit outdoor activity and conservation club, whose mission is "to explore, study, preserve, and enjoy the natural beauty of the outdoors . . . ." Based in Seattle, Washington, the club is now the third-largest such organization in the United States, with 15,000 members and five branches throughout Washington State.

The Mountaineers sponsors both classes and year-round outdoor activities in the Pacific Northwest, which include hiking, mountain climbing, ski-touring, snowshoeing, bicycling, camping, kayaking and canoeing, nature study, sailing, and adventure travel. The club's conservation division supports environmental causes through educational activities, sponsoring legislation, and presenting informational programs. All club activities are led by skilled, experienced volunteers, who are dedicated to promoting safe and responsible enjoyment and preservation of the outdoors.

If you would like to participate in these organized outdoor activities or the club's programs, consider a membership in The Mountaineers. For information and an application, write or call The Mountaineers, Club Headquarters, 300 Third Avenue West, Seattle, WA 98119; 206-284-6310.

The Mountaineers Books, an active, nonprofit publishing program of the club, produces guidebooks, instructional texts, historical works, natural history guides, and works on environmental conservation. All books produced by The Mountaineers Books fulfill the club's mission.

Send or call for our catalog of more than 500 outdoor titles:

The Mountaineers Books
1001 SW Klickitat Way, Suite 201
Seattle, WA 98134
800-553-4453
mbooks@mountaineersbooks.org
www.mountaineersbooks.org

The Mountaineers Books is proud to be a corporate sponsor of Leave No Trace, whose mission is to promote and inspire responsible outdoor recreation through education, research, and partnerships. The Leave No Trace program is focused specifically on human-powered (nonmotorized) recreation.

Leave No Trace strives to educate visitors about the nature of their recreational impacts, as well as offer techniques to prevent and minimize such impacts. Leave No Trace is best understood as an educational and ethical program, not as a set of rules and regulations.

For more information, visit *www.LNT.org,* or call 800-332-4100.